Mary McLeod Bethune
by Emma Gelders Sterne

Illustrated by Raymond Lufkin

Copyright

First Published in the United States by Alfred A. Knopf, 1957.
New Kindle, and print Editions published by Ebooks for Students, Ltd. in 2016 and 2019.

Washington, D.C. (202) 464-9126

See our other titles at ebooksforstudents.org.

TO the young people of the South, who hold
history in their joined hands

INTRODUCTION

I first met Mary McLeod Bethane in the summer of 1921 in Atlanta, Georgia. She was presiding over an important meeting of Negro club women and I was an eleven-year-old youngster working at odd jobs around the YMCA where the meeting was held. She immediately captivated me. She was especially wonderful with young people. Her charm, her wit and humor, her oratory, and her indefinable quality of leadership — all these combined to make a powerful impact on those who came to know her.

All of her life Mrs. Bethune was concerned mostly with young people. She founded Bethune-Cookman College where she was eternally busy helping the students develop their minds and their hearts. During the feverish days of the National Youth Administration she was binding up the sore wounds of despair and frustration that years of depression had inflicted on young spirits. And, finally, in her devoted service to her country and the United Nations she was looking down the long corridor of the future trying as best she could to make some contribution to the betterment of the world in which young people would live and work, and grow to maturity.

While the story of a Negro woman rising from the cotton fields of South Carolina to prominent world posts and overcoming many handicaps is a tribute to her own courage and perseverance and faith, it is also a heartwarming story of what can happen in a democracy. In Mrs. Bethune's lifetime significant forward-progress in human relations can be chronicled. This is important for young people to know when there is such competition in the world for the minds of men. The competing ideologies present their wares for all to see and the story of Mary McLeod Bethune is one of America's significant exhibits.

Mrs. Sterne has captured the essence of Mary McLeod Bethune in this delightful book. The life of this woman is a story that needed telling at this time. For the thousands who did not, and now cannot, know her at first hand the book, Mary McLeod Bethune, helps fill the void.

William J. Trent, Jr.
Executive Director
United Negro College Fund

ACKNOWLEDGMENTS

For the facts and background of Mrs. Bethune's life history, I have drawn on published sources too numerous to list, but I feel that mention should be made of Mrs. Bethune's columns in the Chicago *Defender* and the Pittsburgh *Courier*, her articles in the *Journal of Negro History* and the *Negro History Bulletin*, and her essay in the volume *What the Negro Wants*, published by the University of North Carolina Press.

Still, for a stranger—an outsider—to tell the story of Mary McLeod Bethune would have been impossible without the generous assistance of her friends and fellow workers in the educational world, in the National Youth Administration, and in the National Association for the Advancement of Colored People, the National Association of Negro Women, and the National Council of Negro Women. I am indebted to the many people who drew on their store of memories to help me prepare this record of a remarkable woman, and to those who have read the book in manuscript.

Special thanks are due Miss Ella Baker of the Manhattan Branch of the NAACP; Mrs. Esther Bernhart; Dr. L. S. Cozart, President of Barber-Scotia College; Mr. W. C. Ervin, Business Manager of Paine College; Dr. Clark Foreman; Dr. Carleton Goodlett; Mr. Noah Griffin, Field Secretary of the NAACP; Mrs. Mame Mason Higgins, former Dean of Women at Bethune-

Cook-man College; Mrs. Inez Jackson; Dr. Marguerite Johnson, of the staff of the New York City Board of Education; Mr. John Killens, author of *Youngblood*; Miss Louise Laney; Mr. Edward R. Rodriquez, Director of Mary McLeod Bethune Foundation; Mrs. Charlemae Rollins, Children's Librarian at the Hall Branch of the Chicago Public Library; Mrs. Eleanor Roosevelt; Mr. William J. Trent, Jr., Executive Director of the United Negro College Fund; Mr. Aubrey Williams; Mr. Ernest Wilkins, Assistant Secretary of Labor; Mr. Henry Winslow, teacher and literary critic for The Crisis; Mr. Rollins Winslow.

I am further indebted to the librarians of the New York Public Library and especially to the curators of the Schomberg Collection; to the librarians of the Chicago Public Library, Hall Branch, the San Francisco Public Library, and the San Jose Public Library; and to the librarians of Columbia University, New York City, the University of California at Berkeley, Stanford University, Palo Alto, California, San Jose State College, San Jose, California, and Talladega College, Talladega, Alabama.

In addition, I also wish to make acknowledgment of my indebtedness to the following publishers and authors: Langston Hughes, for permission to quote from "Let America Be America Again" from *Poetry of the Negro People*, published by Doubleday & Company, Inc.; The University of North Carolina Press, for permission to quote from *What the Negro Wants* edited by Dr. Rayford Logan; J. B. Lippincott Co., for permission to quote from *They Came in Chains* by J. Saunders Redding; The Citadel Press, for permission to use material from *A Documentary History of the Negro People* by Herbert Aptheker; Paul R. Reynolds & Son, for permission to quote from "I Have Seen Black Hands" by Richard Wright from *Poetry of the Negro People*, published by Doubleday & Company, Inc.

For editorial and secretarial assistance I am grateful to Mrs. Doris Fuller, Mrs. Louise Kellogg, Mrs. Frieda Graham, and lastly to my daughter, Barbara Lindsay, for her research and perceptive criticism, which went far beyond the usual editorial assistance.

E.G.S.
San Jose, California
March, 1957

Contents

1: The Chain of Human Events

THE FIRST LOOK at the world that Mary remembered was from the high, bristly back of Old Bush, her father's mule. Mary was five years old, plenty old enough to do a share of the family work. The plowing would go a lot faster, her father said, as he lifted her up close to the collar around the old mule's neck, if somebody smart like Mary were guiding the mule straight in the furrows.

"The good Lord knows every minute saved is a help to get our cotton in the ground," he said, in that low, throaty voice of his that was like church music.

The little girl straddled the mule and fastened her fingers tight around the ropes that came out from the bit in the animal's mouth.

"When I say 'Gee,' you pull on the rope to the right hand, nearest the house, that is. When I say 'Haw,' you pull towards the swamp," her father said. "Then we'll drive a straight furrow all the way to the road."

Mary stared around the dusty, sun-warmed field, and at the weathered walls of her house. On the roof, she could see the patches of new yellow shingles her father and the boys had put on last winter to keep out the rain. She could see smoke curling toward the swamp.

So that's where smoke went—to the swamp! The forbidden swamp, a tangle of misshapen cypress trees, weaving light and shadow that was all mystery and wonder. Even Mary's grown sisters ventured only to the very edge of the swamp, and then just once in a while, in the early spring, to bring back root herbs Granny needed to brew her medicine. And fistfuls of purple rooster-head violets.

When Will went to the swamp the way he had this morning to set his rabbit traps, Mama went about her work tight-lipped and anxious until she saw him coming home again, crossing the field in the dusk. If we didn't need rabbit meat so bad, Mary guessed, Will wouldn't be allowed to go at all. If he was home today he'd be walking in front of Old Bush, pulling the guide rope, and Mary wouldn't have had the chance to be sitting where she was, helping her father.

But someday, she meant to go into the swamp and clear through it, to see what was on the other side! She meant to go up and down the road, too—farther than the store, farther than the big house where Mama went to carry the white people's clean clothes home every Saturday.

Mary's gaze left the distant swamp and swung back to the stamped-down earth around the door. The yard was always a busy place. Mary spent most of her waking time there, minding the babies. Her father was always threatening to plant that ground into cotton, too, but Mama wouldn't let him. With nineteen people living in a three-room house, Mama said, you had to have a yard to spill out in. Besides, where would she have her clothes kettle to boil clothes? Where could she hang the clothes to dry? Where could all the family work go on that the house had no room for? Where could they sit on hot summer evenings? Where could the little children play? Just the mention of plowing up the yard for cotton got Mama riled up, worse than the time the hens got in the new-planted turnip patch.

Mary could see her mother already hanging the white people's clothes on the line. Pink dresses for the little girls, white shirts for Mr. Wilson. She was hanging up Pa's other overalls, too—patched, Mama said, with everything but a turnip patch.

Mary could look down on the top of young Sam's head, as he sat on the front step eating a biscuit. Breakfast was over long ago. Chores, breakfast, and morning prayers all had to be got out of the way before sunup. But Sammy was the oldest. He worked out, at the livery stable in Mayesville, and didn't have to get such an early start. He didn't have to be at work till an hour after sunrise. Rebecca and Sally were already halfway down the road on the way to their cook jobs.

"Someday," Mary whispered vehemently, "I'll be grown up, too, and work out and bring home fifty cents a week."

She straightened up and her eyes met those of her father. She hardly ever saw his face that close. Mostly her view of her father was just his muddy, run-down shoes and his legs like tree trunks, or his strong black hands folded in front of him at the family prayers. But she was as tall as her father now, sitting on the back of the mule.

His eyes were looking at her, smiling a little. "You all right up there?" he asked.

"I'm all right," Mary answered, and waited while her father stepped back and grasped the wooden handles of the plow. . . .

But Mary McLeod Bethune's life story doesn't begin with that day's plowing. It doesn't even rightly begin with the day she was born. Where is the start of it? Where should the account of this great American woman have its beginning?

Three hundred years back, perhaps, in Africa? In 1619 when the slave-catchers began their careers of capturing Africans and bringing them to be sold as chattels in the American colonies?

"They came in chains," writes the historian J. S. Redding, "and they came from everywhere along the west coast of Africa—from Cape Verde and the Bights of Benin and Biafra; from Goree, Gambia, and Calabar; Anamaboe and Ambriz; the

Gold, the Ivory and the Grain Coast; and from a thousand nameless villages inland. They were, these slaves, people of at least four great races—the Negritians, the Fellatahs, the Bantus and the Gallas—and many tribes whose names make a kind of poetry: Makalolu, Bassutas, Kaffir, Koromantis; the Senegalese and the Mandingos; Ibos, Iboni, Ibani (like the parsing of a Latin verb), Efik and Falahs, the Wysyahs and the Zandes. Native villages ran red with their blood. The plains and the valleys of Africa rang with their cries. Chained to each other, neck and foot, under the stroke of the merciless sun and the whine of the slaver's whip, the terrified Negroes were driven to the coast."

At that time, one branch of Mary McLeod's ancestry ruled as tribal chiefs somewhere in the vast area known as Guinea. They continued to rule, undisturbed, for another hundred and fifty years. But more and more slave-traders kept landing on the African coast to herd men, women, and children into their ships' dark holds, and deliver such as survived the voyage to the Americas to be sold as slaves.

All this time, until about the year 1776, Mary's mother's people quietly raised their cattle on the gaunt, golden pastures of Africa. They sat under the "palaver" tree, judging and ruling the villages, following long tradition. The house they lived in was stately, their dress on ceremonial days was of the finest.

Then slavers descended on the village and white hairy hands fastened chains on arms that had worn bracelets of ivory and gold. Mary's great-grandmother was brought to South Carolina and sold to a family setting up a rice plantation near the coast. Her husband died on shipboard before the voyage was over.

"I come from a long line of despots," Mary McLeod Bethune joked, in her later years, when someone at Bethune-Cookman College complained that she was too bossy.

Certainly Africa and the history of a proud, capable people brought to ruin cannot be left out of her life story. Taken from widely separated parts of the vast continent, with different languages and customs and no bond or union except the condition of slavery, most of the Africans were cut off from their former life as completely as if they had died. Families were broken up. Men and women from different tribes were thrown together on one plantation. Often the only language in which they could communicate with each other was the English of their masters. Clothes, food, religion—everything was changed. A wall was raised, shutting out the traditions, the very life they had known in their African homes. But Mary McLeod's great-grandmother was of stubborn stock. She did not forget who she was, or where she had come from.

It was to the advantage of the slaveholders that the memories be blurred. It was easier to keep people from rebelling against the conditions of slavery if they ceased to remember freedom, if they could be made to believe that their present way of life, however miserable, was better than they'd known in "savage" Africa. And it was easier for the gentlemen and ladies who lived off the work of slaves to quiet their own consciences if they came to believe that all Africans were barbarians, something less than human.

Religion entered in, too. The idea took hold that the condition of slavery was good if it saved the souls of the heathen. So Christianity, the very religion that teaches that all men are brothers, was enlisted to belittle the African past. (The slaveholders couldn't foresee that the same Bible in which they found the words to support slavery would provide the words to make dreams of freedom come true.)

Mary's great-grandmother, the daughter of an African ruler, received the teachings of Jesus in her captivity. She was deeply religious and passed on her piety to her daughter, Sophia. But she also told the child, born on alien soil, everything that she remembered about her African homeland. She told of the village life and of the coming of the slavers. "In the fields the grain was ripening," she mourned, "and there were none to harvest it when they took us away."

Sophia was sold away from her mother when she was still a child. She was a very old woman when her granddaughter Mary was born. But Africa was real to her. In her old age she had come to sit by the fire and tell stories her mother had told her and sing songs in a language whose words even she scarcely understood.

To the day of her death, Mary McLeod Bethune proclaimed her pride in being African. But her roots were deep in America, too.

At about the time that her great-grandmother was being offered on the auction block in Charleston, South Carolina, three men sat in a room over a bakeshop in the city of Philadelphia. John Adams, a lawyer from Boston, the patriarch Ben Franklin, and Tom Jefferson from Virginia had been delegated by the members of the Continental Congress to draft a declaration to let the world know why the three million people on the Atlantic seaboard were prepared to fight for their liberty.

To be truthful, the country was already at war. There remained only to declare for independence. The paper on the table before the three men was in Thomas Jefferson's handwriting. Surprisingly, he had been designated to frame the document.

"When in the course of human events. . . ." The young man read slowly at first, a little hesitantly. He was the youngest, the least experienced of the committee. He had worked all through the night on the preamble and the specific charges against the monarchy in its misgovernment of the colonies. Perhaps what he'd written was after all not what the others had in mind.

". . . We hold these truths to be self-evident, that all men are created equal, that they are endowed by their Creator with certain unalienable rights, that among these are Life, Liberty, and the Pursuit of Happiness."

He read on with more confidence, stopping to change a word here and there. It was plain that John Adams and Franklin approved.

The young man came to the clause against slavery.

"He (the King) has waged cruel war against human nature itself, violating a most sacred right of life and liberty in the persons of a distant people who had never offended him, captivating and carrying them into slavery in another hemisphere or to incur miserable death in their transportation. The Christian king of Great Britain determines to keep open a market where men should be bought and sold. . . ."

(In South Carolina, an auctioneer was droning: "What am I bid for this strong healthy wench? Fresh cargo, lately off the Schooner Millicent. What am I bid?"—Mary McLeod's great-grandmother was up for sale.)

But in the room at Philadelphia, John Adams shook his head. Ben Franklin pushed back his chair and slapped at a fly on his shirtsleeve. Adams and Franklin had not expected this. Thomas Jefferson was a Virginian, a slaveholder. Neither Adams nor Franklin had ever owned a slave. Both hated slavery, but... a clause condemning slavery would start controversy in the Continental Congress. They wanted to make it easy for all the delegates at the Congress to sign the document they were about to present. Georgia and South Carolina were doubtful. So was New York. It was important to have unanimity.

Besides, they argued, mention of the outrageous slave trade was unnecessary. It was implied in Jefferson's preamble . . . All men are created equal, equally entitled to life and liberty ... It is unthinkable that a nation founded on this principle, they said confidently, would permit one human being to own another. Logic and reason will demand that slavery disappear. But for now, nothing must threaten the unity of the colonies.

Tom Jefferson drew a line through the offending clause. This was the only major change in the document he had prepared. Yet this compromise in the name of "unity" set a pattern at the expense of the enslaved Negro which was to lead the new nation into tragedy.

Mary McLeod's great-grandmother knew nothing of what went on in that room in Philadelphia. Few of the 239,000 Negroes on the continent were aware of the clause that was stricken from the noble document. But over the country many heard the Declaration read from the steps of public buildings and at village crossroads. All probably heard the bells that rang for liberty. They asked themselves (some even asked aloud): "Are the liberty bells ringing for me?"

The slaves did not need a document to arouse the deep craving for freedom. Before the Revolution, history records more than twenty-five insurrections in the Southern colonies, inspired by the human love of liberty. In the North a number of petitions for freedom were presented to governing bodies. "Members of the church of Christ," wrote one group in Massachusetts in 1774, "how can the master and the slave be said to fulfill that command, Bear ye one another's Burdens. How can the master be said to Bear my Burden when he bears me down with the heavy chains of slavery. . . ." Three years later, the very words of the Declaration of Independence were invoked in a petition for freedom: "Petitioners . . . have in common with all other men a Natural and Unalienable Right to that freedom which the Great Parent of the Universe hath Bestowed equally on all mankind. . . ." During the seven years of the Revolutionary War, four thousand American Negroes enlisted and fought in the Continental Army. For the most part, they were freemen from the Northern colonies. But hundreds of slaves enlisted with the consent of their owners. And in every Southern city, Negroes who had managed to purchase their freedom were profoundly influenced by the promise of the Declaration. They joined their fellow Americans in the struggle to make a new kind of nation.

In one way or another, the African captives and their American children, free and enslaved, showed their faith in the words of the Declaration of Independence and supported the American struggle. There was some justification in their faith. One state after another in the North proclaimed emancipation. Vermont began it in 1777. By the turn of the century, every slave north of Maryland was free.

True, the two hundred thousand Negroes living in the South were still considered property. And the Southern Abolitionists were persuaded to put off the problems of emancipation. But during the war and for the next decade, the lot of Southern slaves improved.

The laws against teaching slaves to read were ignored. In the towns and on small farms, many were taught to read and write and to keep household accounts. More slaves were allowed to earn money to buy their freedom. Their skills in farming and crafts were used more freely.

It is true that on the huge tobacco and rice plantations where the largest number of slaves were employed, conditions had improved only slightly. But rice and tobacco crops were becoming less profitable. It was believed that with profits gone, the excuse for slave labor would disappear. Slavery appeared at an ebb tide.

But children of slaves could still be sold away from their mothers. Mary's great-grandmother had borne two sons. One had died. A slave-trader bought the other. The institution of slavery might be coming to its end, but the woman who had lived like a princess in Africa stood on American soil watching her son with chains on his legs, go off in the coffle of captives.

In 1787 delegates assembled for another convention, this time to adopt a constitution whereby the nation would be governed. Thomas Jefferson was not a delegate to the Constitutional Convention. He was in France on behalf of the American states. But his friend and neighbor, James Madison, was one of the leading delegates. The two men had agreed that the moment to end compromise on the question of slavery had come. If the promise of the Declaration of Independence was to be fulfilled, the new constitution must include a clause abolishing slavery.

But again the statesmen compromised at the slaves' expense. The best that the anti-slavery forces could do was to set a limit to the time slaves could be imported. In 1808, the slave trade could be stopped. Time and public opinion, it was believed, were on the side of liberty for the Negro.

Then, at the time when Sophia, Mary's grandmother, was born, something happened to make slavery worth preserving at all costs. The cotton gin was invented. The entire future of American history was changed by the invention of this small wooden instrument to take the seed out of a boll of cotton.

Now, with a few hundred acres of cotton and some "black field hands" bought cheap from the rice plantations or imported from Africa, a man could make a fortune. Three hundred thousand human beings were brought to be sold in the deep South between 1794, the year of the patenting of the cotton gin, and 1808, the year when the United States Government had pledged to stop the traffic in slaves.

And the Negroes themselves? Those in the North who had won their freedom? Those in the South who had built new hopes on the promise of the "unalienable rights" of Life, Liberty, and the Pursuit of Happiness? Of the five hundred thousand Negroes in the United States, not more than one thousand had a vote. But they did have the right of petition. Petitions for emancipation poured into Congress. They did have the right of free speech and free press. Those who were free spoke for their brothers in chains. Those who could write, wrote broadsides against slavery. They did have the right of assembly. Public meetings were held in the North. Negro ministers in the South spread the gospel of freedom straight from the Bible. Songs of freedom were on the lips of the oppressed.

The cotton-planters felt a fear for their possessions. The aristocratic society riding on the backs of the slaves trembled for their beautiful white-pillared mansions. Talk of freedom had become a sickness, they felt.

So they practiced "preventive medicine." New slave codes were passed in the legislatures—old laws against the teaching of reading were renewed and strengthened. Every community in every slave state had its patrol of state militiamen or private guards.

Under the colonial government, before the Revolution, South Carolina had had a law which stated that "any person whatsoever who shall hereafter teach or cause any person of color, slave or former slave, to be taught to read and write, or shall use any slave as scribe in any manner of writing whatsoever, such persons shall forfeit the sum of 100 pounds."

This law, a dead letter for twenty years, was revived. To the fine was added a penalty of six months' imprisonment. Laws were passed against the movement of slaves on the highway, against assembly.

But it seemed that the whole world was conspiring to destroy the peace of mind of Southern planters. The slaves of Santo Domingo rebelled against their masters. Frightened refugees took ship for Charleston. Then-arrival put the slave-owners of South Carolina in a panic. The American experiment in self-government had proved contagious. In France, Life, Liberty and the Pursuit of Happiness was translated into *Liberty*, *Equality*, and *Fraternity*. The monarchy had fallen. A Republic had been established. With a logic the South Carolina planters abhorred, the French had proclaimed freedom for the African slaves in their West Indian colony of Haiti.

The French had repented of their act, it was true. The Rights of Man gave way to the Rights of Empire. But slavery did not return to the island of Haiti. Under the leadership of Toussaint L'Ouverture and later of Jean Jacques Dessalines and Henri Christophe, the former slaves from Africa fought a successful war for freedom.

Again, refugees with their slaves sailed into the safe ports of the United States. Again the slave-owners shuddered. What had happened in Haiti could happen in South Carolina. Repressive laws redoubled in severity. News from Haiti was kept out of the papers. The mails were closed to literature from the North. Curfews were declared. Patrols were placed upon the roads.

But no measures were repressive enough to keep the name of Toussaint L'Ouverture secret from even the most remote backwoods plantation. Even the ten-year-old slave girl, Sophia, sold to a planter out in Sumter County, knew that somewhere on an island, a black man had burst his chains and ruled on a mountain top. She thanked the God her masters had said was the protector of the poor, the oppressed, the downtrodden.

Two hundred thousand Africans were smuggled into American harbors in the five years after the law against importation of slaves went into effect, three hundred thousand in the five years following. To plant and cultivate cotton required a vast amount of cheap labor. What could be cheaper than a slave who was paid no wages and given only enough rough food and clothing and shelter to support life; who could work, and give birth to more slaves?

It is probable, though we have no record, that Mary McLeod's father's people were among the slaves smuggled into South Carolina at this time. (We do know that her ancestry was wholly of African origin. This was a point of pride to her throughout her life.)

Thomas Jefferson, an old and dying man, saw the bonds of slavery tightening. "I pity my country," he said, "when I remember that God is just."

In the next decade there were heartbreaking attempts to throw off the bonds. The whispered names of Gabriel, of Denmark Vesey, and Nat Turner were added to the names of Toussaint L'Ouverture and Henri Christophe when the Negroes talked in the slave-quarters. In the year Nat Turner planned rebellion and died, Sophia gave birth to a daughter whom Mr. Wilson, her owner, listed in his record book by the name of Patsy. Sophia had been on the Wilson plantation for only two years. She had borne three other children, but Mr. Wilson had not seen fit to buy them when he bought their mother. Where her beloved off-spring were, under what masters, Sophia did not know.

The father of the girl cradled in her arms had been born in Africa. He hadn't lasted long on Mr. Wilson's plantation. Too proud to suit, he'd been sold to the first slave-trader who came through Mayesville.

In a week Sophia would have to go out in the fields again. She intended taking the baby with her in a basket. That way the little one would be safe. She gripped the sleeping infant close. "Please God, let me keep this little baby."

Patsy, who was to be the mother of Mary McLeod Bethune, stirred and waked. She was a puny baby, wrinkled and scrawny. She was beginning life a slave and the child of slaves. But her daughter, Mary, was destined to be born free.

2: Born Free

SOMETIME in the 1840's, in Sumter County, South Carolina, five miles out from the village of Mayesville, a big, black-skinned youth called Sam was strolling down the road. He had a note to deliver to the Wilson plantation. The folded paper sticking out of his pocket was probably an invitation to Sunday dinner or some other festivity, for Sam's master and Mr. Wilson were good friends as well as neighbors. Mr. Ben Wilson had the biggest house in Sumter County, but Mr. McLeod had the best hunting dogs, so that kind of made it even.

With the note, Mr. McLeod had given Sam a pass so he wouldn't have any trouble with the patrol. A slave wasn't allowed on a public road unless he could prove that he was on business for his master. Sam couldn't read the name on the outside of the note or the hastily written pass. He didn't know a single colored man who could read and write. But he'd heard there were plenty in Charleston and up North.

Not all the white men who rode on patrol could read either. Just last week a smart colored man was "following the Drinking Gourd," the stars that pointed the way northward. He met up with the patrol before he could hit the woods on the path to freedom. When they stopped him and asked for his pass, though, he was ready for them. He showed them a letter his girl had got for him out of the master's trashbasket and walked on, bold as brass, out of the House of Bondage. He knew the patrol couldn't read any more than a bluejay.

Sam chuckled. He loved to hear stories like that. To hear about escapes to the Underground were comforting, even if you hadn't any intention of taking the freedom road yourself. Not yet, anyway. But it made you feel more like a person, somehow. Somewhere that man, as black as you, was crossing rivers wide as Jordan, meeting freedom face to face on the farther bank.

There wasn't any regular Underground station in Sumter County. Just once in a while somebody would take a crazy chance and make it. Or something terrible would happen to make a poor soul run away and hide in the swamp. And then, more times than not, the bloodhounds would track him down. Sam had heard the hounds baying in the swamp. He didn't want to hear that sound again. Praise God, he'd never had a feeling strong enough to take that risk. Since the day he was born he had been on the McLeod place. Folks brought in from out of the county said it was better here than on most plantations. Sunup to sundown the work went on, but Sam didn't mind work. And the master was easy-goin' as long as you didn't break any rules.

The truth is, Sam loved the land he plowed and sowed. Short of being free, he asked nothing nicer than to see the earth yield the green shoots and red blossoms and then the white bolls from cotton seed his hands had put in the ground.

Two men came riding toward him down the road. White men. Their nags trotted on by. Nobody bothered him, but in spite of himself Sam's heartbeats quickened. That's the way it was when you weren't free . . . you never could forget it, never get it clean out of your mind. It got under your skin worse than chiggers . . . here he was, a great strong man, must be twenty years old, in a sweat because he passed a couple of white men riding down the public road.

Sam came in sight of the big, spread-out house where the Wilsons lived. He walked along the driveway, past the sweet-smelling jasmine, and came to the back door. In the dooryard, stirring clothes in a kettle, was the prettiest girl he had ever seen. She was little and wiry and her skin was as black as his own. And when she smiled, it was like sunshine through the trees.

"I'm Mr. McLeod's boy. I got a message."

The girl nodded and came forward on bare feet with quick, easy steps. "You're Sam," she said.

"How'd you know?"

The girl smiled again. "I seen you at camp meeting last Easter. Heard you singing. I'm named Patsy. Don't work around the big house as a general rule. Mistress brought my Mama in from the fields to do the washing, on account of the regular laundress is ailing. Brought me along to help Mama."

Sam understood that Patsy didn't want to pretend to be a house servant when she wasn't. That was honest of her, and modest.

"I'm a field hand too," Sam mumbled. "Don't know why Master picked me to fetch the note."

Patsy took the piece of paper and disappeared through the kitchen door. When she came back, she was carrying a gourd of cool water for Sam, as if she knew he'd still be standing there rooted to the spot. "Reckon the good Lord had a hand in you bringing the letter," she said slowly.

"Reckon He did." Sam knew without more words that she felt about him the way he did about her.

He ran all the way back to make up for the time they'd stood talking—the ten minutes it took for him to fall in love for life.

Sam broke rules boldly after that. He slipped off whenever he could, to go to the slave quarters at the Wilson plantation, to sit on a split-bottom chair in front of a cabin door and talk to Patsy and to Sophia, her mother.

The third time he slipped out of bounds, he got caught. Mr. McLeod himself was coming home from somewhere or other and saw him crossing the fields. Late as it was in the night, Mr.

McLeod took off his broadcloth coat and got a whip. But instead of baring his back to receive the lashes and standing quiet to take his punishment, Sam spoke up.

"I been down courtin' Mr. Wilson's Patsy, Master. We—we wants to get married," he said half humbly and half defiantly.

Marriage between slaves, even on the same plantation, was illegal, but it happened. Of course, it couldn't be taken very seriously when one or another, the husband or wife, were apt to be sold to another owner any time. And marriage between slaves on different plantations didn't make sense at all. It was out of the question.

But Sam was a good hand, and Mr. McLeod prided himself on being a good master. He showed the measure of his "goodness" now. He laid aside the whip and put his coat back on.

"Courtin' Wilson's Patsy, is it? And wantin' to marry her too, boy? Well, I'll tell you what I'll do, Sam," he said. "I'll see if Ben Wilson is willing to sell the girl and what he'll take for her. Then I'll let you earn the money to pay for her. I can use another hand on the place anyhow. I'll hire you out at the lumber mill. You'll have to have a pass so you can walk to the mill and back before dawn and after dark. It's only three miles down the road. And any money you bring in for over ten hours a day, I'll put aside to buy the girl. When you've brought in enough so I can pay for her, you can marry."

Sam walked the six miles and hauled lumber fourteen hours a day for two years. The purchase price was paid and Patsy became—not free, not even the property of the man who worked for her out of his great love, but a McLeod slave. The offspring would be McLeod slaves, too, to be raised on the plantation or sold.

The Wilsons and the McLeods were pleasantly amused by the romance. Mrs. Wilson gave Patsy one of her old dresses for a wedding dress and at Christmas time, when all slaves had a holiday, they held a real wedding. And Mrs. Wilson reminded Patsy that she ought to be mighty grateful that the McLeods were such kind people. She wished some of those Yankee Abolitionists could see Patsy all dressed up like a bride!

So the parents of Mary McLeod Bethune were married. Both of them worked in the cotton fields every day, except that Patsy had a week or two off every time she had a baby. As the years passed, Patsy hardly ever saw her mother, and that was a sorrow. There was the constant worry, too, that as the children grew older they would be sold away from her.

Their oldest daughter, Sally, was fourteen when the War came. Mr. McLeod went off to fight and Mrs. McLeod, always sickly, let the plantation pretty much run itself. When they were alone at night in quarters, Sam and Patsy talked about Mr. Lincoln's soldiers. There was a rumor that some of them were black like themselves—wearing blue uniforms. Free Negroes. But no soldiers, white or black, came to Mayesville. Nothing much happened, and they couldn't get any real news, just crumbs the house servants picked up from the talk at the big house.

The first year and the second they plowed and planted and chopped cotton. They picked the crop when it was ripe and took it to the gin. And all the while they talked about what they'd do if freedom came to South Carolina.

Then, on the first day of January 1863, news of the Emancipation Proclamation leaked out. The white people called it a joke. But there was open rejoicing in the slave quarters. That very night, Sophia walked over without a by-your-leave from the Wilson plantation, carrying a little wooden chest with all her possessions. She found Sam and her daughter on their knees in thankful prayer.

Patsy and Sam had ten children, all of them alive, all of the family together. Now, none could be sold. Nobody could separate them. This was what freedom meant to Patsy. God was good.

Some of the McLeod slaves went off down the road next day, carrying babies and bundles in their arms or dragging rickety homemade wagons behind them. They had no special destination, no plans except to get away. Being able to move was the test of freedom. Sam and Patsy did not join the ragged throngs on the highways. Sam watched them go, penniless, homeless, with nothing to eat, no shelter from rain or cold. Sam was a careful man, and freedom, now that it had really come, was the thing to be planned for.

Patsy was tempted to urge Sam to pack up when she heard, a year later, that the Union Army was forty miles away at Columbia and was feeding the freedmen and opening schools in tents where you could learn to read and spell. To have a Bible and read the blessed words was worth some hardship.

But with ten children and another on the way, taking to the road did not seem practical. Sam was a farmer. He didn't know anything but farming. You can't plant and harvest, wandering on the road, he argued. So they stayed on at the McLeod plantation in their dirt-floor cabin overflowing with children. Everything got a little shabbier and fewer and fewer acres were planted in cotton. Patsy and some of the other women planted scraps of land in vegetables to feed themselves and their families. Some of the fields grew tall in wild grass and black-eyed Susans.

There was a five-acre piece between the road and tho swamp that used to grow good cotton. When the War ended and Mr. McLeod came back from the Confederate Army, Sam spoke to him about it.

Freedmen all over the South were expecting and hoping the Government would allot them abandoned farm land. But Mr. Lincoln was dead and things didn't look so good. Sam thought he'd better try to buy.

"Sell you land, with no cash down and whatever you can spare to make payments with from year to year? That wouldn't be very good business, Sam. Anyhow, it's against the law. You wouldn't know about the Code, would you? The State of South Carolina doesn't aim to have you niggers owning land, war or no war. But I'll tell you what I'll do. You and Patsy can stay on here and work. The children, too. I'll feed you and you can keep on sleeping in the cabin. I'll pay you something when I can."

Another year went by. Patsy heard the Black Codes had been repealed. In some places, rumor said, Freedmen's Bureaus were being opened to help people get land. And schools to teach you to read. But Sam had his heart set on that strip of land that used to grow good cotton.

It turned out that piece didn't belong to Mr. McLeod after all. He had just leased it all these years from the Wilsons. Mr. Ben Wilson was the richest man in town. Maybe he would let them have the land. Patsy went herself to the Wilson house.

Mrs. Wilson was in sad need of a laundress. If Patsy would come and work for her, she'd credit her wages for the land.

"When you've worked out the purchase price," she said, "I'll get Mr. Wilson to deed you the field. Sam can cut logs out in the wood lot to build a cabin."

Patsy and Sam had twelve children now, half of them big enough to work in the fields. Patsy went every morning down to the Wilsons'. Sam and the children and even Sophia, old as she was now, worked in the McLeod fields for their keep and for a few dollars wages each year. The money went for little extras above their rations—things like tobacco for Sophia's corncob pipe, and coffee and sugar.

It took four more years for Sam and Patsy to get the piece of land they could call their own. They were years of tremendous change in most parts of the South. The passage of the Black Codes had convinced the Federal Government that the ex-Confederate soldiers intended to keep everything except the form of slavery. A new plan was put into effect. The Fourteenth and Fifteenth Amendments to the Constitution defined the status of the freedmen as citizens, with all the rights enjoyed by other citizens—including the right to vote. The states that had seceded were required to set up state constitutions in accord with the new conditions.

A number of the leaders of the rebellion were disfranchised. All others who had supported the secession were required to take an oath of allegiance to the Constitution—including the new amendments—as a condition of taking part in the government. Federal soldiers were stationed in the states to ensure the enforcement of the laws.

Remote and isolated as they were from the centers of news, the Negroes who had stayed on the plantations in places like Mayesville lived on scraps of overheard conversation and whispered rumors. The Freedmen's Bureau didn't have forces enough to reach out to every little hamlet. Newspapers didn't help, because there was nobody to read them. It was not, for instance, until the summer of 1869 that the people on the

McLeod plantation knew about the Legislature that sat in Charleston.

"A government, they call it! Scalawags and carpetbaggers and niggers makin laws!" Mrs. Wilsons voice was the carrying kind and Patsy, on her way to hang out a basket of wet clothes, stood listening under the open window.

Nigger . . . She brushed aside the hated epithet.

"Please, Lord, let her keep on talking. Let her call us anything she wants to so long as she lets drop news of what's going on. It's not knowing how you mean to bring us on the road to freedom, Lord, that's troubling."

Patsy had a habit of talking to her God—giving advice as well as asking.

"Lord, does Mrs. Wilson mean what I think she means? If our people are taking part in government, it must mean we get a vote. Oh, Lord, I thank you."

But who is it with us, she wondered. *Carpetbaggers and scalawags.* She stored the new words in her mind. Sam would have to search out their meanings. Mrs. Wilson had moved away from the window. There wouldn't be any more news from that source.

Patsy flung the wet garments one by one over the clothesline. They flapped like flags in the breeze—flags of freedom. She stuck clothespins on helter skelter, in a hurry to get home, to get back to the McLeod plantation before dusk.

"Sam, you take a nickel and go down to the crossroads store," she commanded. "Mama ain't had no smoking tobacco for a week. Go buy some. But don't just buy and leave. You get old Mr. Hawkins to talking. Find out who scalawags are—and carpetbaggers. He's bound to know."

The store, a mile away on the Sumter road, had more empty shelves than it had goods. Sam fumbled as long as he could, picking out a little bag of tobacco and waiting for the other customers to finish their trading and walk out the door.

Sam wasn't a talker like his wife. It was a marvel to hear the way Patsy could bandy words around. But they had to find out about this new government. It was part of freedom to get to know.

Mr. Hawkins opened up real easy. "Carpetbaggers? You darkies sure are ignorant. That's what everybody calls the folks from up North. Freedmen's Bureau men and such are carpetbaggers. They ain't so bad, just a little uppity. And scalawags—people like the Wilsons and the McLeods that swear they'll die before they take the oath of allegiance to a constitution that's got the new amendments in it, they call the rest of us scalawags. All I say is, if there's going to be government, I prefer to have my say in it. They can call me names if they want. And as for lettin' colored people vote—well, if we got to do it, we got to, that's all."

Sam's lips were dry with excitement. He ran his tongue over them before he spoke again. "Mr. Hawkins, sir, you sayin' we can vote?"

"What do you think the amendments were for, the Fourteenth and Fifteenth that stick so in Old Man Wilson's craw? The Federal Government says you darkies are citizens. What's more, they got soldiers to prove it."

"Where's the voting? How do you get to do it?"

"Up at Sumter—But you get along now, black boy—" Mr. Hawkins had heard the front step squeak. Another customer was coming in. It could fair ruin his business if they saw him exchanging conversation with a black field hand. To be called scalawag for having taken the oath was bad enough. To be suspected of being a nigger-lover would be plumb ruinous.

Sam understood. He picked up the bag of tobacco and tramped up the road singing in his deep bass. *Rise and shine and give God the glory . . . glory for the Year of Jubilee.*

Next Sunday the whole family walked to the outskirts of Sumter to the pine-board church Reverend Bowen had built. It was five miles there and five miles back, carrying lunch and the new baby. They didn't get to go often but it was worth the walk both for the blessed words Reverend Bowen read from the Good Book and for the way he recited those Amendments afterward, under the sycamore tree, with lunch all spread out and even the children listening wide-eyed.

Reverend Bowen could barely read himself, but he never faltered as he recited word for word the precious promise.

The right of citizens of the United States to vote shall not he denied or abridged by the United States or by any State on account of race, color, or previous condition of servitude.

"The Lord has been good to us," he said. "Over in Charleston they've voted for schools and a hospital for the sick. They've done away with whipping posts. Can't nobody go to jail for debt. Lawmakers, white and black together, have done these things. Behold how good it is for breathren to dwell together in unity."

"Amen," Sophia responded, as if they were back in the church.

The Reconstruction Legislature, composed of "scalawags and carpetbaggers" and freedmen, for all their inexperience, founded the first public-school system in the Southern states, "without discrimination between white and black." They spent a great deal of money and went into debt, but it was for roads and railroads, schools and almshouses and hospitals. There was inefficiency and waste, but for the vast majority of people in South Carolina there was a great new hope. Eight thousand former leaders of the state were disfranchised but one hundred thousand people for the first time could call themselves men and citizens.

The material benefits of the Reconstruction governments were slow to spread out from the cities to places like Mayesville. No schools had been built in Sumter County, no new roads or public buildings.

Still, in 1870, a man like Sam could walk to the courthouse with a piece of paper in his hand and come out with it registered—a deed to five acres of land. Sam came out of the courthouse with a last name, too. A white man from the Freedmen's Bureau had explained about needing a surname. Sam could have chosen any he wanted. He'd been "McLeod's Sam" for all his thirty-odd years, though, and McLeod seemed as good a name as any. He hoped Patsy and the children wouldn't mind bearing the name of the man that had owned them.

(It never occurred to Sam McLeod to wonder where his adopted name came from or what its history was. If anybody had told him that fifty years later a daughter of his would be entertained in a Scottish castle by Lord and Lady McLeod, he'd have said they were crazy. Or he'd have shrugged off all the trappings of title and asked: Were those other McLeods God-fearing and honest? He'd have wanted to know how the crops grew on that land across the water. A last name didn't make Sam McLeod feel more a man. It was having earth of his own to plow, and logs all cut and split to build his house that mattered.)

Sam and his sons pitched in to build the cabin. There were fourteen children now to house and Patsy's mother besides. Sam decided they'd have to have three rooms. And he wanted a wooden floor instead of the earthen floor of slavery. The man at the sawmill where he'd worked so long said he could have a pile of boards that were warped too bad to sell. The clay for the chimney would come from the swamp.

The cabin in Mayesville, South Carolina where Mary McLeod was born

Hauling the lumber and clay wasn't the only problem. Sam needed a mule in the worst way. You could hardly raise cotton without a mule to pull the plow.

"You remember Old Bush on Mr. Wilson's place?" Sophia said to her daughter. The old woman hadn't set foot on the Wilson plantation since Emancipation, but she could call every animal, every rock, and every tree to mind. "He so balky, Gabriel's trumpet wouldn't move him when he get his feet set. Rest of the time, he a right good mule."

"He'd do," Patsy answered and, without telling Sam, she went down the road to the Wilsons' again and bargained to do their wash at so much a week to pay for the mule and a plow and a rickety wagon.

The family moved into their house to begin a new life —a life of toil and poverty, but a life of self-respect and deep happiness.

The fireplace did for a cookstove. The beds were the same straw-filled pallets they'd always slept on. Mr. McLeod let them take those from the slave cabin. He let Sam take the old rocker, too, the one that had been in the barn. Sam made some benches and a table big enough for half of the family to eat on at one time. These were their furnishings, these and Sophia's chest, and a shelf above it. The shelf held the kerosene lamp which had been Patsy's wedding present sixteen years ago.

The younger children were asleep in the back bedroom, worn out with the excitement of getting settled in a new home, when a knock at the door surprised the family only a few days after they had moved in.

"Why, Reverend Bowen! Come right in," said Sam warmly.

"Get Reverend Bowen a drink of spring water right quick, Sally," Patsy ordered. "That's a long walk out from Sumter. We're precious proud to have you, Pastor."

"And I'm proud to see our folks digging in and building homes on their own land, Sister Patsy. You and Brother Sam are the first in the congregation to have your own house, built by your own hand. It seemed to me that this house should be especially blessed. So I bring a gift for your home."

Neither Patsy nor Sam could say a word as they looked at the black-bound book their pastor offered them. Neither of them could recognize a single one of the gold letters on the cover. They didn't have to. To have land, to have a home—and now, to have a Bible that was truly their own ....

Reverently, Patsy placed the Bible on the shelf, next to the kerosene lamp.

It was Sophia, seated near the fire in the old rocker, who spoke for the family. "Praise the Lord, for the earth is full of the goodness of the Lord!"

It was a year after Sam's first cotton was ginned before he got to vote. In 1872, the night of the voting, a dozen men in red shirts paraded by his house on horseback. They didn't stop. They didn't do anything. But Patsy, awake and understanding, knew that the freedom road stretched far ahead. She got up and turned the leaves of the Bible she couldn't read. God was on their side anyway. He who holds the waters in the hollow of his hand.

Three years later, into this family, with this history, a fifteenth child was born, a girl. On July 19, 1875. They named her Mary, a good Bible name. Mary Jane McLeod.

Patsy lay on her pallet in the front room by the fireplace and watched her mother bathe the new baby. How good it was, bearing a child under your own roof, in freedom!

"She's a homely child," the grandmother said as she wrapped the infant in a scrap of cotton blanket. "Not anyways pretty, but she's strong."

"And born in freedom," Patsy said.

Sam came in from the fields and looked at his daughter.

"She's free," Patsy repeated.

Sam was not much of a talker. "Part-way free," he said, thinking of the Red Shirts and the white-sheeted Klan that was being whispered about over the country. And he got down on his knees next to Patsy's pallet. "Let us pray."

3: Mary's Year of Jubilee

THE NEGROES in the South called 1863 the year of Jubilee, because, on January 1 of that year, Lincoln issued the Emancipation Proclamation. Along the roads, around the camps of the Federal Army, in the cities, in the slave-quarters, it was all hope and talk and singing. It was families being reunited whose members had been sold apart. It was learning to read in Army tents or churches or in shacks or city basements. It was the hope of land and a plow and a mule to draw the plow. It was "Thank you, Mr. Lincoln . . ." Jubilee Year!

But Mary McLeod's Jubilee Year didn't come until almost a quarter of a century later. By the time she was born, in 1875, the hopes of land to be allotted had faded. The short-lived Freedmen's Bureau had been abolished. Hard times had hit the whole country.

Before the Civil War, the slave-owners had owned labor and land and capital. After the war, they still owned the land and what capital there was. Their one thought was to make sure that the former slaves would continue to work on terms of their choosing.

A South Carolina Congressman, a Negro, said in 1875: "We do not ask for any legislation for the colored people of the country that is not applied to the white people. All that we ask is equal laws, equal legislation, and equal rights throughout the length and breadth of this land."

But the gap was too wide. For too long the slaveowner had told himself that his slaves were not men like other men. He had come almost to believe it himself, or seemed to, if the evidence of his actions can be believed. By the time Mary was three years old, the government of South Carolina was back in the hands of those who intended that the white South should do the ruling while the black South did the same work they had done in slavery.

Not until much later in life did Mary know the full details of how this was done. Mayesville—probably because it had received so few benefits of the Reconstruction years—also saw little of the violence of the overthrow. No schoolhouse was burned, because none had been built. No homes were looted of furniture and books and pictures, because no Negro there had succeeded in making more than the barest living. At voting time, the mysterious, white-sheeted night riders—the Ku Klux Klan—were on hand, but they did little more than parade and burn a few crosses at night, after the child had been crooned to sleep in her grandmother's loving arms. And the Klan was not so mysterious to women like Patsy who washed for a living. An extra sheet in the laundry after a night of parading told its own story.

When Mary was old enough to go berrying, she noticed empty shacks by the road on the big plantations. Her big sister allowed that some more families must have hot-footed it to Kansas. But Mary had no idea where Kansas was or why fifty thousand former slaves had left the South and moved there.

One family had moved to Mayesville some years before. Amelia, the little girl, was in Mary's Sunday school class. On the Fourth of July, just before Mary was six, the church held a picnic in a grove near Sumter. On the way to the picnic the McLeods walked by Amelia's house. Mary started to run ahead to fetch her friend. Patsy stopped her.

"Not today, honey," she said. "Not on the Fourth of July. It's their day of mourning." Then Mary saw that the door was shut tight and the shutter closed on the window.

The family were refugees from the trouble at Hamburg, down on the Georgia border. Seven years before, on Independence Day, the people at Hamburg had been celebrating. Federal soldiers—a Negro company—still stationed there were parading. Before night what had been a joyous parade turned into something else. Before the trouble ended, the violent mob of "Red Shirts" led by a Confederate general and by the man who was now the governor of the state had burned half the colored people's houses in Hamburg. The whole town was left desolate and most of the families had "refugeed" to other parts. Amelia's family got along all right after they fled to Mayesville. But on the Fourth of July every year they stayed indoors. Their neighbors understood and respected their feelings.

Patsy explained to Mary matter-of-factly and briefly. She liked to spare the children all she could. If bad things had happened, if all the hopes of Jubilee Year hadn't come into being, they still had each other and their house and freedom. God's ways were not the ways of man and there was no use getting Mary stirred up over what couldn't be helped. Not on a beautiful Fourth of July on the way to a picnic ....

But Patsy couldn't always stand between her little girl and life as it had to be lived. Late that fall, one Saturday afternoon, when it was time to take the big basket of laundry to the Wilson home, the big boys had gone fishing. Patsy decided to carry the clothes herself, but the basket was awkward for her to carry alone, especially now when she was again big with child. She scrubbed Mary up, put on her clean dress, and let her go along.

Mary couldn't have been more pleased. She trudged along the dusty road, carrying one end of the basket and shooting questions at her mother a mile a minute. It wasn't often any one of the children had their mother all to herself. Not with fifteen in the family!

When they came to the big house, the two Wilson girls were in the back yard, playing paper dolls. They had a little playhouse nearby, all painted blue, with glass in the windows. They took Mary inside and let her touch the dolls and the tea-set and showed her how the little iron cookstove really worked.

It was all nice and friendly until Mary picked up a book. It was lying open at a table with a picture on the page and some words in big black letters underneath. Maybe these friendly little girls could read. Maybe . . . A great surging hope rose in Mary's mind. She carried the book carefully across the playhouse room.

"Which is A?" she asked. "Show me a A."

The book was snatched from her hand and slammed shut. "Don't you touch that book with your black hands! Don't you know reading is for white folks? You can't never read . . . you're black."

Mary ran out of the house and out of the yard. Her mother found her when she came out with the money and the basket full of dirty clothes for next week's washing—found her face-down by the side of the road beating her heels up and down and sobbing.

"How come, Mama? How come?" she said, over and over on the way home.

Patsy could not answer. In the first days of the Reconstruction, the law establishing common schools had been passed, and the word had gone through the state like a fresh breeze blowing. Illiteracy among the slaves and the free Negroes had been ninety per cent. Now, in 1882, almost half the counties had a school of some sort for four months a year, supported either by state funds or by churches and public-spirited citizens in the North. But Mayesville belonged to the neglected half. Illiteracy among the colored people in this little crossroads town was one hundred per cent. Patsy had long ago given up hope of learning to read her Bible herself. She had watched the older children grow up without even expecting an education. Now here was Mary—wanting the one thing her mother couldn't give her.

"Maybe the good Lord'll find a way for you, Mary," she said comfortingly.

There wasn't much time in Patsy's life to think about it after that one bitter afternoon. She had too much to do just keeping her family fed and clothed and washing for the Wilsons and helping Sam in the fields.

But Mary had time. When she helped with the cotton-picking, she compared the white cotton with her black fingers. She began to hate the whiteness of the bolls. But her anger only made her pick faster and harder. She'd show people, some day, that black hands could hold a book.

She knew that colored people did read somewhere, far off away from Mayesville. But right here . . . "Reading is for white folks . . . You're black!" The September sun burned the words deep. Those white girls could read while she could not.

"Just give me a chance," she whispered as she moved up and down the long rows. "Please, Lord Jesus ... in a special way . . . ."

October, 1886 . . . Mary walked along the dirt road toward the corner store. She was tall for her eleven years and carried the heavy sack of hickory nuts over her shoulders almost as easily as a man. The sun came down, lighting up the red sweetgum leaves, making magic colors in the columns of dust that hung over the road. The smell of fall was in the air. Mary felt good.

Mr. Hawkins was measuring out the lard and sugar she'd get in exchange for the nuts. Nobody else was in the store.

"That colored preacher was in from Sumter way last week," he said. "Left a message for your maw. Seems there's a mission school starting out beyond the railroad tracks. School for colored. He said your maw would like to hear about it and I said sure, I'd tell you. Don't see myself why some folks are so dead set against you-all getting an education."

A school! Mary sang all the way home, swinging the tin of lard. *O, don't you hear those bells a-ringing, ringing for the Year of Jubilee* . . . The school would be three miles away, but she could walk back and forth. . . . Rise and shine and give God the glory . . . Six miles a day would be nothing compared to learning to read. . . . *Glory for the Year of Jubilee*!

But when she came in sight of their own house a doubt struck her. Could she be spared? This was a matter for the whole family to decide. She was an important breadwinner. Since the day she was five years old and sat on the back of the mule to speed the plowing, she'd been her father's helper. Last year and the year before, when she was just nine, she had picked two hundred and

43

fifty pounds of cotton in a day. None of the boys, even when they were home, did much better than that. And Kellie and Will had already gone to Atlanta, and Sammy worked at the livery stable. Maybe her father couldn't do without her. Maybe Mama couldn't either, with the new baby. . . .

That night, after prayers, they talked it over. After all, Sam said, with doubt in his voice, the cotton was already at the gin. This winter he aimed to clear a piece of the swamp to plant a little rice . . . that was work a man could do alone, he guessed ... if Mary was so bent on reading.

Granny puffed at her pipe and rocked her chair. "She's bent on amounting to something, Sam. Can't you see this child is a child of freedom? Big as a woman, strong as a man and only ten, eleven years old. This child'll learn to read, praise God, and come home to read us all the Bible. Blessed be the name of the Lord."

School had been going a week when Mary stood in the door of the unpainted wooden building next morning. Children were streaming through the door and taking their seats on the rows of benches. A big iron stove was getting red from the burning wood inside. One of the big boys brushed past Mary with a load of hickory logs in his arms.

"You want any more wood, Miss Wilson?" he said to the teacher sitting up front at a table.

Mary looked at the young woman in the white shirtwaist and dark-blue trailing skirt. The teacher! Her skin was a light brown. Her hair, brushed tight into a knot, was black. Yes, she was colored, as Mary had expected —though not blue-black pure African like herself. Not many colored people were.

But that boy had called her "Miss Wilson." Mary had never heard a colored person called by anything but a first name before. She had never heard anyone of her own race given the dignity of a title.

She puzzled about it all that first wonderful morning as she sat at the place assigned her.

"Miss Wilson, can I get a drink?" "Miss Wilson, how do you spell Abraham Lincoln?" "Miss Wilson, Tommy's got my slate pencil and he won't give it back!"

All around her, the other scholars seemed to take for granted that you called a colored lady *Miss*.

Calling a person by a title like that showed you respected them. . . . Grown-up people ought to be respected ... if they were good, that is. . . . Someday, Mary decided, she'd have people calling her by her name with the proper handle. "Miss McLeod." . . . She whispered it to herself and sat up a little straighter on her bench. *Miss, Mrs., Mr.* —they were little words. It didn't take long to say them. If white people hoarded them for themselves, never used them to black folks, there must be a reason. "Was it just a way of keeping us from feeling like human beings? Was it to 'keep us in our place?'"

They wouldn't let Mama learn to read . . . and they never called her anything but Patsy even if she was older than they were. It was a little thing, but important, Mary decided.

"Someday," Mary said to herself, "when I'm grown up, I'll be Miss McLeod, and if I'm married I'll be a Mrs., called so by colored and white. That's the way things ought to be."

Almost fifty years later, in 1934, Mary McLeod Bethune was a delegate from Florida to the first meeting of the Southern Conference for Human Welfare. White and Negro men and women sat in the same hall in Birmingham, Alabama, discussing ways to make the South a better place to live in.

A resolution for better schools was proposed. Mrs. Bethune offered an amendment. It was voted on and passed. The white woman who was chairman of the meeting was forward-looking and sincerely concerned. She meant well, but never in all her life had she called a colored person by anything but a first name.

"Mary's amendment is accepted," she announced, with a gracious nod in the direction of the dignified black woman sitting on the front row just across the aisle from the wife of President Roosevelt.

Slowly Mary McLeod Bethune rose and addressed the chair. "Madam Chairman," she said, "my name is *Mrs.* Mary McLeod Bethune. The secretary will please be instructed to record it so."

The room rocked with applause. Another step had been taken toward the promise of the Declaration of Independence. One more barrier between white and Negro had gone down

Mrs. Bethune sat down again, a little surprised at the ease of her victory. She had simply spoken what she believed was right and probably didn't remember that first day at school when the belief came to birth in her mind. But the use of proper titles in the South today, at least in public places, if not in private relationships, is a small memorial to Miss Emma Wilson of the Presbyterian mission school at Mayesville, South Carolina.

4: Blue-Back Speller

THE THREE MILE walk to school every morning was like an exploring expedition. Mary's eyes darted from one side to the other to spy out any edibles growing along the roadside or in deserted overgrown orchards. Once she had taken her place on one of the nine benches in the schoolroom she put everything except the day's lessons out of her mind. But when school let out, and she started home with her empty tin bucket swinging on her arm, she started gathering dandelion greens and herbs, wild fruits, and nuts she had noticed on the morning journey. She rarely came home without a full bucket. That way, she figured, the family didn't lose her help as much as they might have.

One time she carried a bundle of clothes to Mayesville for an old woman who lived near the school and the white woman gave her a dozen setting eggs as pay. Her mother borrowed a setting hen to hatch them and by spring there were young chickens pecking in the yard. Sam had bought a cow from a family that was moving to Columbia, so they ate better than usual that year.

In the first weeks of school Mary sat on the front benches with the beginners. After a month she moved back steadily. At the beginning of the second term she was on the back bench with a boy whose father had gone to one of the "Army tent" schools in Charleston and so had been able to teach his son to read and spell. There was another girl in the class who could read more fluently than Mary. Her father had a barber shop in Sumter. He had escaped to Canada before the war, but had returned after Emancipation and had brought three volumes of Frederick Douglass's writings back with him in his trunk. He lent these, one by one, to Miss Wilson, to read to the scholars, along with the Bible.

With none of the advantages of these two students, by the beginning of her third year of schooling Mary was helping Miss Wilson teach the newcomers. At numbers, she was better than any of the boys.

One reason for Mary's quick progress in her school work was her regular attendance Though the school term lasted only four months each year, many families kept their children home any time there was work to do. Plowing time, hog-killing time, the boys would stay out. Sometimes they'd even slip away to go hunting. Some girls stayed home if they didn't have a nice dress to wear. And always there was sickness. But Mary was never sick, and Patsy McLeod saw to it that she was not kept at home for extra work. Nothing but ripe cotton to be picked would have tempted Mary to miss a day in the schoolroom and, of course, cotton-picking time came during the long vacation when Miss Wilson was back in North Carolina at Scotia Seminary.

As soon as she could spell out a few words and understood the miracle of the alphabet, Mary began teaching her younger sisters, Hattie and Margaret. She urged her grown-up brothers and sisters to let her teach them, too.

"My boss at the livery stable can't read so good himself," Sammy objected. "How long you think I be working if he thought I knew more than him?"

Sally laughed. "Sammy's right," she said. "You ought to hear my people at their dinner table talking about the foolishness of having schools for us. Mary ought to make herself a long dress and get a cook job. Smart as she is, she could make two dollars a week right away, and get a husband, too."

Sally was going to marry the Wilsons' coachman at Christmas time and live over the coachhouse, or maybe go North to work. They hadn't decided.

Patsy rarely raised her voice in anger, but she did so now. "The people you work for are not *your* people, Sally McLeod," she said tartly. "Your people is right in this room. Mary's going to school as long as I can keep her there. You let Mary alone. She's different from any of my other children and she's going to have her chance."

Granny nodded. "Different, bless God. Mary, get down the Bible and read us a piece while I help your mama with the ironing."

"I can't read the long words yet," Mary answered, fingering the leaves of the Book hungrily. "But someday I will."

At Christmas time, Mrs. Wilson gave her two servants a wedding in her parlor. She gave Sally a new dress and a gaudy kerosene lamp to put in the room over the carriage-house, and let her take home the wedding cake to her family.

Surprisingly, much as Sophia loved good things to eat, the old woman wouldn't take a bite of it. "Too much like slavery times," she murmured. "Do you mind, Patsy, how the old master give you and Sam a wedding? After Sam bought you with his hard-earned pay. He'd bought you but you wasn't free! After the wedding, Mr. McLeod claimed you, and all those years you borned children, not knowing when they might be sold away from you. Like they sold your brothers and sisters, Patsy, till I didn't have none left but you."

"Miss Susie mean to be kindly, Granny," Sally protested.

"Looks like even in their kindness they want to make slaves of us again, without the name of slavery. What's a little old wedding cake? In Africa, my mama said, the family feasted three days running. ... In Africa they killed a whole cow at a wedding."

Usually, when Granny began talking about the past, Mary listened eagerly to every word. But just lately she had heard something in school that disturbed her. Miss Wilson said the Africans were poor heathen. They knew not God and had not the comfort of Jesus. The missionary societies sent over good people to bring the gospel to the Africans, so they could be saved and go to Heaven.

"Someday," Mary said, "I'm going to Africa. I'm going to be a missionary and bring our people to Jesus."

"You got the 'somedays' again?" Sally teased, but once more Patsy interrupted.

"I told you Mary is different. She's going to have the somedays till she dies."

A year later, Mary could read the Bible whenever anybody asked her. No longer need Patsy take the Book down from its shelf just to finger the pages. She had a daughter who could read!

At the close of the school term that year, Miss Wilson let Mary take her blueblack speller home. The young girl had a reason for wanting it. It came to her that she could teach her mother to read the Bible herself. Patsy was more than willing, and for several nights she puzzled out the letters of the alphabet by the light of the kerosene lamp.

"A," Patsy repeated after Mary, "that's like in Adam. . . . B . . . Blessed are the meek. . . . C, that's the first letter of the Christ Child."

But before they had come to the letter D, Patsy, worn out with all her labor and the seventeen children she had borne and raised up, was asleep. Mary did not try the reading lesson again. The speller, wrapped in brown paper, was put beside the Bible on the high shelf, there to stay until the end of vacation.

She had better luck showing her father how to figure his cotton when the bales were weighed in to be sold. She could tell, before the weigher named a figure, what the cotton ought to bring.

One Sunday, after dinner, the family was sitting out on the stoop in the cool October sunshine, when two white men rode up to the yard. They had small farms down the road and Sam was on good terms with them. Yet Mary could feel her father tighten up in every muscle. Too many bad things had happened to colored families when white men came riding to the door.

However, all that these men wanted was to find out if it was true that Sam's girl Mary could read and do number work. They hoped it was, because they suspected that the man down at the gin was short-changing them and they'd like to find somebody who could figure up the account.

After that, others came to get Mary's help—white and black. It was good to have somebody who could read and write and figure, besides the big planters and the men at the gin. Somebody who could add up your accounts and tell you exactly what you owed. Neighbors kept coming all that winter, and Sam walked around proud as could be, bragging about Mary's learning, that third year of her schooling.

But after the New Year, when the peach blossoms were blooming and the mocking birds were beginning to sing in the swamp, Mary noticed that her father grew silent and glum. A few weeks later, when the frost was out of the ground and planting time was just around the corner, he came in and pulled off his work shoes and sat down by the fire with his head in his hands, like an old man.

"What's the matter, Sam?" his wife asked, her voice sharp with anxiety.

"Old Bush . . .

"Is that mule sick again? Why don't you let Granny doctor it? You know she's got a hand with animals," Mary said, quick with advice as usual.

"Won't do no good. The mule's dead."

That night Mary prayed. She explained to God that they had to have a mule to pull the plow and her pa wouldn't buy another mule on credit. He wouldn't go into debt to a white man. To her pa, freedom meant not to be beholden. . . .

But morning came and there was no answer to Mary's prayer. There was only one thing she could see to do. She waited until after school and then she went to Miss Wilson and told her that she couldn't come any more. Their mule was dead and there wasn't anybody at home except herself strong enough to pull the plow. Her father would have to hitch her up and she could pull while he guided the plow in the furrows.

She even managed a smile when she said good-by to her teacher. "Granny always said I might not be much to look at, but I'm strong as a mule!"

5: Miss Wilson's Miracle

ON A BACK STREET in Denver, Colorado, Mary Crissman, a Quaker seamstress, pedaled away at her sewing machine. In the spring and fall, she went out to sew, spending a few days at a time in the homes of her neighbors, making up bolts of gingham or calico into dresses and shirts, or woolens or silks into Sunday clothes. In between times, she did plain sewing that was brought to her at home in her rented room. Sometimes she was called on to make a wedding dress of ivory brocade ordered from San Francisco or from the East. Or a hand-stitched christening dress for the newborn child of one of the wealthier mine-owners or merchants in town.

She had never married, but she loved little children. And as she worked she often thought of the Negro children in the South, not yet brought to that full freedom that allows human beings to develop themselves in the fullness of the promise of God who made the world. Her father had gone into the South with the Army during the war. Being a Quaker, he wouldn't fight, not even for freedom of God's most forsaken children. But the Anti-Slavery Association had sent him down, even before the Freedman's Bureau was established, to teach the slaves to read and write, to care for their bodies and their souls. He had gone away on his mission the day after Abraham Lincoln's Emancipation Proclamation was signed. That was all he was waiting for. Mary Crissman had been ten years old at the time. She still had the letters he wrote home.

Miss Crissman was pious. She took great comfort in her beliefs and practiced her Christianity as best she could. She went to the little stone meeting-house on Sundays. She "tithed," setting aside ten cents of every dollar she earned to give to the poor, the oppressed, and the heathen. For years she had given her tithe money to many good causes, a little at a time.

In August of the year 1889, when her customers were beginning to ask how soon she could come to them to outfit their children for another school year, Mary Crissman thought of a new plan of giving. There is no record of how the idea came to her. The inspiration might have come from a human-interest paragraph in *Godeys Lady's Book*—a story about the struggle of the Negroes to continue the education started under Lincoln's armies and under Reconstruction governments. Surprising bits of information often appeared in the fashion magazine, sandwiched between patterns of bustled skirts and shirtwaists with leg-o'-mutton sleeves. Or it may be that, at the homes of her customers, the middle-aged seamstress read in the home missions columns of the *Presbyterian Review* of the need for education in the South. The reasons for Mary Crissman's decision are buried in obscurity. Yet what she did that midsummer afternoon in Colorado changed the lives of many people over the continent and continued in its influence long after she was dead.

She sat down and wrote a letter to a small Presbyterian boarding-school for daughters of freedmen, offering to send her tithe money to provide a year's schooling for some Negro girl— "one you are sure will make good." The letter was addressed to the principal of Scotia Seminary at Concord, North Carolina.

Since Scotia was supported almost entirely by contributions from individuals or church groups outside the South, Miss Crissman's letter was one of several in the mailbox at the Concord post office. Nevertheless, it excited the interest of Dr. Satterfield, the headmaster, and of the half-dozen former students staying at the school in vacation time. It was rare that one contributor was willing to take full responsibility for a scholar. And the seamstress from Colorado had left the choice of the new student to the school.

A week later, Miss Emma Wilson, who had, as usual, been spending her free time at her old school, boarded the railroad train for Mayesville, South Carolina. She had Mary Crissman's letter in her skirt pocket and, folded carefully inside the envelope, enough money to pay for a ticket from Mayesville back to Concord.

No one met Miss Wilson at the depot because she wasn't expected back so soon. It was cotton-picking time, and the school term would not begin until the cotton was ginned and baled. She asked the baggageman to keep her valise because she had a four-mile walk ahead of her.

As it turned out, however, the young schoolteacher got a ride for most of the way in a mule cart, so she arrived at the McLeod farm before sundown. The whole family was out in the field, bent over the rows of heavy-headed cotton. All the family, that is, who were still left at home. Sally had married and gone. And the older boys had gone, too. There wasn't much on a five-acre farm to hold them.

Mary saw Miss Wilson coming across the dusty field, stepping carefully between the cotton rows. Coming, maybe, to say the new term was beginning? But it wasn't any use. Mary prayed every night to ask God to help her find a way to finish her studies so she could go to teach His Word to her kin in Africa. But how could she? They didn't have a mule yet, any more than they had in the spring.

As her teacher's trim figure came closer, Mary's mind darted down a dozen trails of thought. Maybe Miss Wilson wasn't coming for her after all, but for one of the little children. Maybe, when the cotton was baled and sold, there'd be enough money to buy a mule. But then there was the debt to the white man at the bank, for her father, in spite of all his determination, had had to borrow. And Granny wasn't getting any younger. Mama would need help with the ironing if Granny's health failed. ... It just wasn't any use for Miss Wilson to be coming around.

"Short of a miracle," Mary said to herself, with unaccustomed bitterness, "my schooling is done with."

Patsy McLeod got up off her knees and went toward the visitor; but Mary kept on picking cotton. She didn't look up from the row until she heard her mother calling her name in a voice like a jubilee.

"Mary! Your teacher chose you! The school chose my girl to get the scholarship. Come here, every last one of you, while Miss Wilson reads the letter again. Mary's going to Scotia!"

There were Miss Wilson and Mama hugging each other and laughing and crying over the news in the letter fluttering in the breeze. And her father and Granny and the girls crowding around, and the little ones hanging onto Miss Wilson's skirt with their grimy hands.

But Mary just stayed on her knees where she was in the cotton row and prayed to God in thankfulness.

Many times in the years to come, in her writings and on the lecture platform and in conversation with friends, Mary McLeod Bethune spoke about that moment in her life. To her it was proof of victory through prayer. And the faith that her teacher had that she was "one who would make good" was a talisman, a treasure, a foundation rock to be added to her family's faith in her. On this was built the faith in herself which many people believe to be the key to her character.

"I believe, first of all, in God, and next of all, in Mary McLeod Bethune," she said years later. Some thought her vain with pride, because she believed so confidently, so joyously, first in her God, then in herself. Yet her faith in herself was built upon the belief *that she was one chosen to advance the welfare of her people* to bring nearer reality the American dream. And, as Rollins Winslow put it, "operating under this very credo, she launched and won many frontier battles in human relations."

There was no more cotton picked at the McLeods' that day. Miss Wilson stayed to supper. Granny killed one of the frying-size chickens and cooked it, crisp and golden. Patsy made up a pan of biscuits while Mary churned a fresh batch of butter. Then she went to the spring across the road for a bucket of cool water.

The short walk in the dusk alone under the still branches of the live oaks gave Mary time to think about the change that had come in her life. She was concerned about her family. How would they manage without her? Winter time wouldn't be so bad. With her gone, there'd be one less to feed. But plowing time would come again. Maybe she oughtn't to go at all. But that was unthinkable. Her mother wouldn't let her give up the scholarship. Neither would her father, though he didn't drive for knowledge the way Mary and her mother did. Freedom was her father's driving force—the freedom that lets a human being take from life what his spirit needs. He knew that Mary wanted learning the same as he wanted to make his land yield a crop. As long as her father had his two hands, he'd plant seed and make a harvest—whether anybody was there to help or not.

Walking back with the water sloshing in the wooden pail, the girl considered her home almost with the eyes of a stranger. Or with Miss Wilson's eyes. The schoolteacher was kind and good, but she was not from this part of the country. She'd never known what it was to be poor-slave poor. She, likely, was wondering how they all managed in such a little place. Twenty souls there used to be, counting Granny, when all the McLeods were living at home.

Yet they hadn't felt very crowded. It was easy, if you didn't have many possessions. Pallets to sleep on weren't like having a lot of beds. Pallets could be rolled up in a corner of the back room in the daytime. If everybody had just two garments apiece—one on his back and one in the washtub—you didn't need wardrobe room. There wasn't room for enough chairs or benches around the table where they ate. But that was all right because they didn't have dishes enough for all the family to eat at the same time anyway. Granny had her rocker by the fireplace, and the two cane-bottom chairs were good to sit on when they weren't being used to prop up the ironing-board. Outside of those, there were homemade benches and the floor. Anybody that didn't feel like sitting on the floor, could fetch a stump from the wood pile to sit on.

Looking at it piece by piece this way, Mary had to admit the McLeods didn't have much in the way of a house. But yet it was better than some the white farmers lived in. It had a floor. It was so clean that Reverend Bowen used to say Sister Sophia and Sister Patsy must have a soap factory hidden somewhere behind the cow shed.

Mary stopped to change the bucket to her other hand and noticed that the persimmon tree was loaded with a good crop this year. She'd have to remember to warn little Hattie again not to chunk the fruit down until after a frost. She'd pucker her mouth, for sure. Hattie took a lot of looking after and lately she'd turned to Mary more than to her mother. Hattie would miss her when she went away to Scotia and she'd miss Hattie. Hattie was bright. Maybe, someday, Miss Wilson would take her in the school. Mary had never given up hope that some of the family beside herself would get an education.

When she got back to the house, her father and Granny and Miss Wilson were sitting at the table eating supper, and Miss Wilson was telling what the school would be like. The rest of the family were clustered around in silence, all except Hattie and the baby, who were gnawing the chicken wings on the back step. The rest of them would eat later. There might not be much chicken left but there'd be plenty of biscuits and gravy and buttermilk.

After family prayers were over, Sam went over to a neighbor's house to ask for the loan of his mule and cart to drive Miss

Wilson out to Reverend Bowen's home, near Sumter, where she always roomed during school term.

"I'll have to stop at the depot to get my valise," Miss Wilson said. "And before I forget, I'd like to give you Mary's railroad ticket to Concord. Though I'll see you again before she leaves."

Patsy took the ticket and laid it between two pages of the Bible up on the shelf. There it would be safe and come to no harm.

"When do you want she should go?" Patsy asked.

"A month from today," the schoolteacher said. "If you can get her ready by then."

Get Mary ready! Miss Wilson's words seemed to linger in the air long after the squeaking cart had gone down the road. Granny settled back in her rocking-chair and lit her corncob pipe. She sucked away at the stem without speaking. Patsy didn't say anything either. But, as she cleaned up the supper things, she rattled the tin pie-plate dishes and her lips were pressed close together in a way she had when she was worried or anxious.

Finally, Mary spoke. "What did Miss Wilson mean get me 'ready'?"

Becky came in from milking the cow in time to hear the question. She set down the milk pail and the lantern she'd used to see by.

"You might be book smart, Mary McLeod," she said, "but you don't seem to have no common sense at all. There's more to going away to school than a railroad ticket and a letter. There's clothes to put on your back and something to carry them in. You saw all that extra ironing Mama did for little Miss Essie last week. Fluted ruffled drawers and starched petticoats and dressing-sacks with ribbons run through. Miss Essie going to Charleston to boarding-school, that's why. And when I carried the basket of clothes home there was a dressmaker from Sumter stitching on a sewing machine in the back room and Mrs. Wilson scurrying around with dress goods on her arm, matching colors."

'That's white people's way," the grandmother interrupted sharply.

Patsy sat down wearily. "White people's way or not, Mary's got to have some good clothes to wear so far from home. It would shame me to let her go shabby. It comes at a bad time, too. A little later and the cotton would be sold. We'd have a little money for cloth and such, after paying the storekeeper and getting the flour and meal and sidemeat."

Mary shook her head emphatically. "Money from the cotton isn't going on my back," she said. "It's for a mule. I'm going to Scotia for learning. I can study my lessons without shoes and stockings. I can wash one dress while I've got on the other, same as always. Miss Wilson didn't choose me for pretty. She don't expect I should carry along any finery."

Stiffly, Sophia raised herself from her chair, and moved toward her little wooden chest where she kept her things. She had brought the chest along with her when she came, the day after Emancipation, to make her home with Patsy and Sam. That was more than twenty years ago and she had never let anybody see the the bottom of it. But whenever need got beyond a point, it seemed the old woman would open her chest and pull out something to help out. The blanket Mary was wrapped in when she was born had come from the treasure chest. So had the button string she had played with as a little child.

Hattie and little Maggie drew close, now, to watch the lid raised. Sophia pulled out a length of linsey-woolsey cloth, the kind the Wilson slaves always got for Christmas. She pulled out a spool of thread and four pearl buttons and handed them to Mary.

"I been saving this cloth too long as it is," she said. "It'll make a good dress and us has got plenty floursacking for underwear. The Lord means you shall have an education and He means you shall be dressed fitting for His work. You ain't pretty but you're a good girl to look at. You fix up the best you can and respect your body as you do your soul. And all of you quit fretting. Mary's going to that school in a manner that won't disgrace her. The Lord will provide."

As Mary McLeod told about it long afterward, the Lord did provide, through the willing hands and good hearts of the neighbors. When the news got around the McLeod girl was going to North Carolina to get more schooling, neighbors knitted stockings. They sewed pretty aprons. They brought dresses they could spare— or said they could spare—for Patsy to make over. And Mr. Hawkins pulled a pair of brown high shoes with copper tips off his shelf. He'd had 'em, he said, since before the War, and they were too shopworn to sell. He wasn't like some folks. He liked to see colored people trying to better themselves. Sam was welcome to the shoes for his girl if she didn't have something better.

The end of September came and the day Mary was to take the train to Concord. Everybody in the neighborhood came down to the depot to see her off. In wagons, on mules, in oxcarts and afoot, they made a regular procession through the streets of Mayesville to see Mary get on the train.

Most of them had never been on a railroad train themselves but they hadn't come out of curiosity just to see the train go by. They had come because Mary McLeod already was becoming a symbol to her people. She was moving ahead on the path of freedom. Here at last was one of their own, going off to a big school to make something of herself. Maybe a teacher, maybe a missionary . . . Some predicted one thing, some another. But each of them shared in her victory over almost unsurmountable obstacles. Each had a share of the miracle. Each felt renewed hope in the promise of America while they waited at the depot for the northbound train to come in.

No doubt the stationmaster was a little dismayed to see all the country carts pouring in, taking up space at the hitching posts. Was Mayesville going to be subjected to one of those mass exoduses he'd been hearing about? There'd been rumors floating about that colored people were leaving the state in droves. They'd better stay where they were and not go running off to the North or to Kansas where they'd freeze to death. Had some agitator slipped into Mayesville stirring up trouble? He was scarcely less disturbed when he found out that all the hubbub was just because a black girl in a linsey-woolsey dress was going off to North Carolina to school. Education were sure to give the colored people the big head and make 'em feel as good as if they were white.

He stood in the depot door and scowled. But he didn't try to order the crowd away. There were too many of them together. Anyhow the train was due in five minutes. . . .

As the time grew close, the neighbors drew away, leaving the family to cluster around to say good-by. But Miss Wilson, who had come in from Summit, stayed a minute longer. She explained once more that a teacher from the school would meet the train in Concord. Mary was not to worry. She was just to take a seat in the cars, put her bundles on the floor and give her ticket to the conductor. The trip would take eight hours. She would be in Concord before dark.

Then Miss Wilson put a lovely plaid shawl around Mary's shoulders, because, she said, it got colder in Concord than down here. "You write a letter," she whispered. "I'll take it to your mother. And I'll write letters, too."

"Yes, ma'am," was all that Mary had time to answer. But the school teacher's promise lifted a load from her heart.

The inability of members of loving and close-knit families to communicate with each other when they were separated by distance was one of the tragic features of slavery. It was one of the saddest results of the Southern program of illiteracy in the period when Mary McLeod was growing up. Miss Wilson's thoughtfulness meant that the bond between Mary and her family need not be broken. There could be letters between them. She would know how the planting was going in the spring—how the mule her father was bargaining for worked out—whether Granny's new rheumatism medicine did any good. Above all, words could flow between herself and her mother. Someday, maybe, there'd be time for Miss Wilson to teach her mother to read!

"You heard what Miss Wilson said?" Mary held the thin, bony shoulders of her mother in her strong arms. The engine roared in with a rush of air. She had to raise her voice to be heard. "I'm going to write you all about Scotia. And about the train ride . . ."

The brakes screeched and groaned. The train hardly came to a stop before Mary's foot was on the car step. She remembered to wave good-by to the crowd of friends standing at a respectful distance. Sam handed up the bundle of clothes and the lunch Granny had put up and wrapped in an old newspaper. The whistle blew and the wheels began slowly to turn. The shouting, waving, loving people at the depot disappeared from Mary's sight. An era in the life of Mary McLeod had ended. But the love she had been surrounded with went with her always.

"I was shown goodness in my childhood," she wrote. "My parents believed in me. I learned to believe in other people. To be sure I saw trouble and the way was not easy; but I have thanked God and said Glory Hallelujah!"

6: Greek and a Toothbrush

EIGHT HOURS was not enough to savor all the wonders of that first train trip. To this child of a log cabin, the day-coach with its red-plush seats, its polished ceiling, and its spacious glass windows was unheard-of luxury. The only thing like it that she could think of was the picture of Queen Victoria's throne-room that Miss Wilson had pinned up on the schoolroom wall.

She sat primly on the cushioned seat and it seemed to her that the queen on her throne could not be more comfortable. She held onto her bundles with one hand and clutched her ticket in the other until the blue-coated conductor came to punch it. But after the first hour she felt at ease, as if traveling on the railroad cars was something the McLeods did every day.

When she saw an old lady across the aisle open a shoe box and take out a sandwich, she unwrapped her own lunch. Tears came to her eyes. Granny had put in a whole half of a chicken, breast and all. Mary ate every bit of it and licked her fingers. She saw a smile cross the old lady's face.

"First time I ever had enough chicken in my life," Mary said, leaning across the aisle.

She hadn't meant to talk to anybody, especially not to white folks, but before they had crossed the state line to North Carolina she knew the life stories of half a dozen passengers and was minding a year-old baby while the mother took a nap! That was Mary's way. She cared about people and drew them to her always. She never held back her warmth and friendliness out of concern about the impression she was making. She always assumed that people liked her—and generally they did.

The thing that Mary remembered most about that train ride however, was neither the red-plush luxury nor the people. It was the sight of America skimming past her window. It was not the detail of the countryside that engaged her attention, for she knew every tree and bush and flowering weed at a glance. She knew the names and habits and seasons of the moss-hung liveoak, the slick green magnolia standing in front of a half-burned, abandoned mansion, the sweetgum, tawny-red now, storing sap that would make sweet twigs to chew next spring. And she could tell the number of bales of cotton a farmer must have raised, just from looking at a ragged, picked-over field. It was neither the farmhouses nor the little towns on both sides of the railroad tracks that excited her interest; nor the rivers they crossed on high wooden trestles, nor the distant mountains, the color of russet apples. None of these things made her heart jump, looked at by themselves.

It was the largeness, the sweep of her native land. And the Carolinas were only two states in the Union. There were thirty-seven more states, and the Territories, and Mexico and Canada. North America, South America, Asia, and Africa, Europe, and all the oceans—Mary could almost hear Miss Wilson's geography class reciting. She wanted suddenly to see the whole world—God's whole beautiful world. If people knew how beautiful the earth was and all the fullness thereof, how could they ever be mean to one another? It was so wonderfully big—and way off, beyond those everlasting hills in the setting sun, was Miss Mary Crissman, giving her this gift of learning and expecting her to make good. She wouldn't disappoint Miss Crissman. She would make good, all right. She felt it in her bones!

This quality of self-confidence stood Mary McLeod in good stead in her first days at boarding-school. The change in her surroundings was so great that a less outgoing person might have been overawed and confused. But Mary loved every bit of it, from the moment when Miss Rebecca Cantcy, Miss Wilson's friend, met her at the station.

"How did you know it was me?" Mary asked as she walked along beside the teacher, unconscious that she looked in any way different.

Rebecca Cantcy forebore to correct the grammar. That would come later. But she was glad Emma Wilson had suggested that the scholarship pupil from Mayesville come a few days early to get used to the environment of Scotia. Emma had warned the other teachers that Mary McLeod was a raw country girl. It had been a bit of a shock, nevertheless, to see the pigtails, the brass-tipped shoes, the paper-wrapped bundles. Miss Cantcy was glad that Dr. and Mrs. Satterfield were called away from Concord. She had a great admiration for the austere New England couple who had founded the school and were giving their lives to the work of educating the former slaves. But sometimes Dr. Satterfield didn't understand—how could he understand?

She smiled at the girl bouncing along beside her with the awkward energy of an untamed colt. They rounded a corner and Miss Cantcy pointed to a red-brick two-story house set back from the road.

"There it is," she said. "There's Scotia."

The only brick building in Mayesville was the Episcopal Church—for whites only. Mary had never been inside a brick building. She had never walked up a staircase.

Rebecca Cantcy opened the door with a key and led the new pupil upstairs to a bedroom so she could wash up before meeting the others.

It was a small room with two narrow beds. The bedspreads were snowy white. So were the curtains at the window. There were two chairs, a chest of drawers, and a table with a washbowl and pitcher decorated with pink roses. Two toothbrushes stood in a tumbler and two towels were neatly folded over a rod at the side. A small mirror hung above the dressing table and beside it, a colored print of the infant Jesus in the manger. On the other side was a picture of turrets and towers and yellow clouds: Jerusalem the Golden.

"You'll have a roommate, Mary, but Abby Greeley hasn't come yet," Miss Cantcy said.

"A whole room, just for two people!" Mary sat down on the edge of her bed and bounced up and down to feel the softness. She changed her vision of Heaven, then and there. "I used to think Heaven was towers of gold and wings of angels," she confided. "But maybe it's a room like this for every one of God's children!"

When Mary had washed and smoothed her braids, the teacher led the way down to the dining-room. The school term would not begin for several days. Only a few teachers were at the school—the ones who had been there all summer studying and getting the house ready. Miss Cantcy introduced Mary and showed her where to sit.

The table was set with a white cloth like the one Mary's mother washed and ironed every week for the Wilsons. Mary had never eaten at a table like this one, with a place set for each and every person and platters of cold meat and fried mush and little dishes of applesauce—and in the middle, flowers in a vase. Black-eyed Susans. They were pesky weeds in the cotton rows but Mary had always had a liking for their perky faces.

She bent her head while Miss Cantcy, sitting at the head of the table, said the blessing. A knife and spoon lay on one side of her plate, and on the other—a fork. Mary's self-confidence suddenly left her. She didn't hear "for what we are about to receive . . ." She forgot to say Amen. The McLeods didn't have any forks. A spoon or a knife if you needed one, but never any forks. She had heard about forks from Sally, who was always grumbling about having to shine the silver at her cook job. Maybe if she watched carefully, she could see how to hold it and the teachers wouldn't know her ignorance.

But Mary McLeod's innate honesty and frankness would not permit even such a small deception. It wasn't any sin to be fourteen years old and not know how to hold a fork.

She threw back her head and laughed at her own moment of panic. "You'll have to show me, ma'am," she said to the young teacher at her right. "Forks are just for white folks in Mayesville!"

It was like that all the first few days. Everything was different. The iron cookstove in the kitchen that burned coal instead of wood. The lamps in every room with chimneys that had to be polished every morning. The water pumped from a deep well right by the house. And that beautiful room she slept in!

By the time the other girls began to come, though, Mary felt at ease. One or two of the new girls were from homes almost as poor as her own. Mary took them in hand and spared them the awkward shyness which usually made the beginning of a new term at a school like Scotia rather difficult. She had them practicing how to hold a fork, and made the dinner table rock with merriment.

The night before Dr. and Mrs. Satterfield were to return, something happened, however, that jolted Mary MeLeod. The last two teachers came from their homes in the North. The new girls were introduced to them: Miss Chapman and Miss Bowers. Mary put out her hand, then drew it back quickly. The two young women were white!

Miss Chapman, the tall, willowy one, took the girl's rough, work-worn hand in hers. "I'm glad you've come to Scotia, Mary," she said. "Emma Wilson has told us a great deal about you. I think Miss Crissman will be proud of her scholarship pupil."

Next morning, Dr. Satterfield was at the head of the table to lead morning prayers. At the other end of the table was his wife. Somehow, it no longer came as a surprise to Mary to find that they, too, were white.

Classes began that morning. Mary's first class was with Miss Bowers.

"I am from Boston," the teacher began. "I'd like to tell you a story about something that happened to my ancestors a long time ago. It was a quiet night in December, 1773. A British merchant ship loaded with tea rode at anchor in Boston Harbor. Suddenly, some rowboats moved out from the shore. In them were my great-great-great grandfather and his neighbors, determined to have no more tea if it was taxed without their consent as citizens. They opened the boxes and dumped the king's tea into the ocean. They cried: 'Taxation without representation is tyranny! That was a beginning of the American Revolution, a beginning of the struggle for government by consent of the governed. Americans struck out against injustice and tyranny and oppression, just as they have struck out again and again. They said that 'all men are created equal, that they are endowed by their Creator with certain Unalienable Rights.' "

Miss Bowers's people were white; yet they had had to fight for their freedom too. They were oppressed and they struck out. And claimed Unalienable Rights ... Mary didn't know exactly what the word meant. She repeated it to herself several times so she would remember it and find out. Unalienable . . . Whatever it meant, it was a beautiful word on the tongue. And not all white people were the oppressors. Some, like Miss Bowers, remembered even when they had won their unalienable rights that other people still had their rights to win!

Never again would Mary lump all white people together. Those who wanted above all else to "keep the Negro in his place" had done their best to create a wall of hatred and distrust in Mary McLeod. But two young white women who taught at Scotia crumbled that barrier. A half-century later she still remembered.

"Through Miss Chapman and Miss Bowers," she wrote, "I came to understand that there were decent white people who cared about what I was as a person. For that, I have always been grateful."

When Mary entered Scotia College it had been in existence six years. It offered the courses that were everywhere considered proper to a school of higher learning at that time. Colleges for men had always taught "the classics" and "moral philosophy." Colleges offering higher education for women made sure; to include all the same subjects. There were still people who sincerely believed that serious study of anything beyond music and penmanship and a smattering of polite literature would bring on brain fever in the female sex. The colleges had to prove this wasn't true And in spite of the fact that dozens of free Negroes had won degrees from universities in the United States and abroad, the majority of people, north and south, still doubted that the former slaves were capable of any intellectual achievement.

It was natural that schools like Scotia, founded to give the benefits of higher education to Negro girls, should cling to the traditional course of study. It was natural, too, that the students, taught all their lives that they were inferior beings, wanted—and needed—to prove that book learning was not beyond them.

So, at Scotia, the traditional college subjects were taught. And girls like Mary McLeod, only three years removed from illiteracy, doggedly recited Latin verbs and puzzled over algebra problems. In some ways, the classroom and life were far apart. Companionship with the students and teachers, the time to read, the time to think, and even the hours spent in household duties in a well-equipped home were valuable parts of Mary McLeod's education in the years she spent at Scotia. She was never a great scholar, but she learned to use the library to satisfy her unending curiosity. The men and women, the events that were part of her own history, and had up to now been only half understood, passed in review before her. From the first day, when her desire to understand the word "unalienable" led her to the Declaration of Independence, she made the great ideas and language of American democracy her own, as much a part of her as the Bible had been. From the Declaration, her reading led her to the speeches of Lincoln, to Thoreau's letter on the death of John Brown, to Thomas Paine's writings. She thrilled to the stories of one of the older teachers who had been a nurse with the Union forces and knew Harriet Tubman.

In informal talks like this, Mary learned the history of the long struggle against slavery and the history of other countries too. Lecturers came to the school and told what was going on over the whole South—bad things and good. She came to understand, from the lists of men who lost their lives in other parts of the South, why her mother sat tight-lipped but proud when her father went off to the polls to vote on election days and why so many of their neighbors in Mayesville had gone off to Kansas that time when she was just a baby.

Other lecturers came—missionaries going off to save the souls of their brothers and sisters in Africa. Mary sat on the edge of her bench and listened to the frock-coated, eloquent preachers. And she got the "somedays" again, more fiercely than ever. She was awed by these men who were going across the ocean to carry the words of Jesus to the heathen. One thing troubled her, though. They spoke as if all the Africans were savages, as if Africa had no history. As if the judges, the cities, the songs and legends Granny knew about had never existed.

On her first trip home, Mary asked her grandmother why it was the missionaries didn't seem to know more about the way Africa used to be. The old woman had grown very feeble, but her mind was as clear as ever and her tongue as sharp.

"When I was a little thing, size of Sally's girl-baby, I remember a big rock in a creek, down by the slave-quarters. Must have been near Charleston—I don't remember the place. But I remember that rock. My mama used to set me on top of it—it were that big, like an island. But the creek waters kept beatin' against it, crunchin' off a piece here, a piece there. Before I got sold away from there, the drops of water had cut that big rock down to size, the everlasting tiny drops of water. Last time I saw it, that rock wasn't bigger than a pebble. Likely it's gone now altogether."

Sophia, descendant of an African chief, leaned back in her rocker and sighed.

"That's what the white people done to the remembrance our people brought from Africa. They dribbled it away until it were no more than a pebble or a grain of sand. Bless you, child, they *had* to. Even the whites— the most of 'em—have got a conscience. Didn't they receive the word of God straight from the Bible? They know the Bible say all men are brothers. But they want hands to till the fields and dig the ditches and cook their victuals and wash their clothes so they can wear the clothes and eat good and read the Book. They come fetch black hands from the kingdoms of Africa. Conscience say that wouldn't be a brotherly act if the black hands belonged to *men*. The devil whisper: "Make them blacks leave behind all that makes men and women. Make 'em forget all that makes 'em proud." And they done it, bit by bit, like the water crumble that rock. White people never did know about Africa neither, same as water didn't know about the rock it crumble away. But the glory of our people, it were real."

Coming home that summer had a curious effect on Mary. She was like two people—one part of her was bubbling over with eagerness to pour out all she had learned about better ways of living. Another side was suddenly shy.

She saw Granny grown suddenly very old. She saw her parents working year after year without any material change in their lives. Her mother was smaller and thinner than she had remembered, her father more silent. And there'd been trouble and disappointments they hadn't let Miss Wilson write to her about. Last year had been a good cotton year and cotton sold for twenty-five cents a pound. But the bank had called in the loan of any Negro who went to polls to vote. Her father still had a little owing on the new mule he'd bought. He had cast his vote, as always. Then, paying off the little debt had taken all the money from the cotton. So they had gone hungry.

And the white-sheeted Klan was marching again and burning crosses. People were leaving the county almost like the Kansas exodus twelve years ago. Benches in the church were empty. Even if families stayed behind, the young people were leaving. Sammy had gone. So had Sally and her husband.

Mary saw the burdens the people at home were bearing. She didn't want to add to them by new ways that might seem like criticism. She had managed to earn a little spending money, one way or another, and had bought a pocket handkerchief for Maggie, a doll for Hattie, and a string of yellow beads for Granny. Those presents didn't worry her. But she had a pair of house slippers for her father to cover his bare feet when he pulled off his work shoes; and for her mother, a dozen tin forks. And she'd brought toothbrushes for everybody.

Suppose they thought she was belittling those she loved best because they went barefoot and sopped up pot liquor with pieces of cornbread and ate crisp fried pork with their fingers? Suppose they thought she was setting herself apart? For three days, the slippers and the forks stayed wrapped up in her bundle.

Mary was wrong. Her parents were delighted. Not only her own family, but all the little community looked to her to bring new ways from the outside world. A perfect rash of fork-buying broke out until Mr. Hawkins, down at the store, couldn't make out what was happening. And everybody who could get one took to carrying a clean white handkerchief to church.

Before the summer was out the girls and women from a mile around took to dropping by to ask "that McLeod girl" advice about everything from whether boiling; drinking water really made you safe from the fever to how to trim a hat or fix their hair in a pompadour as she did. The yard sometimes had so many people sitting; around that it looked as if Mary were holding class. That gave her an idea. She began to have a class one night a week for anybody who wanted to come—a class in literature and singing. She read aloud, sometimes Bible stories, more often scraps of poetry or things she had cut from newspapers. And she led singing of hymns and spirituals, in harmony, just as Miss Bowers did. Outdoors like that, with no light but the fireflies, it sounded beautiful.

Of course all the visiting stopped when the cotton was ready to be picked. Mary worked, then, from daybreak to dark, in the fields. For the first time, she outpicked her father. After the cotton was ginned, she persuaded her father to dig a well, so they'd have drinking water without depending on the open spring.

She was helping him, working with pick and shovel, when the barber from Sumter and his son came to call. They wanted to talk about colleges. The boy was hoping to go to Fisk University or to Howard.

"I want my son to have the best he can get," the old man said. "To partake of the feast of learning . . . but I heard you had to have some Latin and Greek before you could get in. Where can he get such a thing? I've been trying to teach him some this summer while Miss Wilson is away. But I never saw a book printed in Latin or Greek in my life."

Mary rubbed her hands clean on her skirt and went into the house. She took her Latin grammar out. She hadn't even opened it and the summer vacation was almost over! She had meant to study, to get ahead for next term. But if she lent it to the boy, maybe he'd manage to teach himself enough to enter the doors of a college.

She stood by the door with the book in her hand. To partake of the feast of learning . . . Yes. We have the right to sit at the table with the rest of God's children. The things of the spirit and mind—that's what her mother and Miss Wilson and Miss Crissman wanted to give her . . . what she longed for herself. But decent ways of living, weren't they important, too?

Mary McLeod had not consciously thought out her ideas of education. She had heard the arguments at the dinner table at school over which was best for the Negro race. Howard and Fisk universities on one side—on the other, Hampton Industrial Institute and Mr. Booker T. Washington down at Tuskegee in Alabama. Mr. Washington's school, it was said, taught hardly more than reading and writing, but it did teach work skills and better ways of living. Mary herself had not entered the discussions. The talk about the kind of education her people needed was for people like Abby, her roommate, who cared for nothing but being a teacher. Mary's own mind was set on going to Africa as a missionary.

The summer at home had made a difference. It had given her a set of values—something to go by that lasted her her whole lifetime and in later years influenced many thousands, perhaps hundreds of thousands of[people.

"Education," she said to herself, "it's Greek and a toothbrush. Learning for the sake of learning but learning for life's sake, too."

7. Servant of God

FOR GRADUATION, all the girls at Scotia wore white; white shirtwaists with high collars and white skirts almost touching the ground. The first notes of the *Battle Hymn of the Republic* sounded. They marched across the connecting vestibule to Faith Hall, the school chapel.

Through the dim light filtering in from the stained-glass windows at the side, Mary could see that every seat was filled except those reserved for the graduates. Mary had helped some of the younger girls set up the folding chairs that morning and had fastened the garlands around the speaker's platform. The colors of the rose window behind the platform turned the white blossoms of the smilax garland all the colors of the rainbow. Mary nodded to herself. She was satisfied.

In the years she had spent at Scotia she had developed all her latent love of beautiful things. Faith Hall, filled as it was now with people and song, was loveliest of all.

Some of the parents had come to see the graduation, and townspeople and teachers from other schools had come to hear the singing and the recitations. The hall was full.

Nobody had come to see Mary get her diploma. The railroad fare from Mayesville cost more cash money than her parents saw in six months. She had only managed two trips home in all the years at Scotia.

Though none of her kinfolk were in the crowded hall, Mary did not feel alone. The teachers and the girls had come to seem as close to her as her own family. Besides, graduation from Scotia was not the all-important event to her that it was to most of the girls. With a diploma from Scotia they were ready to take up their chosen careers. But to Mary even this post-graduate work was just a beginning.

She had been at the academy for seven years. Two us ago her own seminary class had gone out to teach, to nurse, to get married. Mary had stayed on for the higher course. Her goal was still to go to Africa as a missionary—a servant of God. At eighteen, she was thought too young. Now she was twenty and it appeared that God—and Miss Mary Crissman—were going to give her the chance she longed for.

Before she walked up the speaker's platform to speak her graduation piece, she felt in her pocket for Miss Crissman's letter. Way off in Denver, Colorado, this woman she'd never seen was saving her tithe money so Mary might have another year's training at the Moody Bible Institute in Chicago. That was

God's way; Miss Crissman, no less than Mary herself, was an instrument for bringing the light of Christianity to the Dark Continent.

Mary stood up, unafraid of the audience of strangers. She was never afraid on a speaker's platform. She knew that she could carry her listeners along with her. That confidence in her power to communicate was probably one reason why she felt the call to be a missionary. Perhaps if she had been a man, she would have turned to the ministry. But for a girl, going to Africa was the way to become a servant of God.

Still, she had ideas of her own about what a missionary had to do. It would not all be preaching and singing, much as she loved both things. She meant to teach the laws of health and cleanliness—good ways of living. She was sure these were needed in Africa just as they were in America. She was going to Moody to learn how to convert the heathen, but she was taking along some pretty definite notions of her own!

No one would have called the tall, big-boned woman pretty. But there was something about her that made even strangers feel more alive in her presence. "Electric" was the word her friends used to describe her—in a time when electricity was a mysterious power that still excited wonder. The girls and teachers alike, even austere Dr. Satterfield, relied on her strength and warmed to her love. She had, it is true, never succeeded in molding herself quite to the ladylike pattern of the Scotia ideal. Her spirits were too high; she had too much life and individuality. But she had done something more important: She had made herself a link between the New England teachers and the girls from Southern cabin homes, the shy uncertain scholars from the backwoods.

She had made herself a link, too, between the school and the people in the town. In order to get the money for things not covered by Miss Crissman's scholarship, and to get a little money to send home, she had worked out —in the fields of near-by tobacco farmers, in white people's kitchens, in a laundry— anywhere she could pick up a few dollars. And everywhere she worked, she broke down suspicion and prejudice against the school. She disarmed the white people with her hot rolls and her singing. They bragged about her cooking to their friends and said maybe that colored school wasn't entirely worthless. She made friends with the colored sharecropping farmers and broke down their suspicion that Scotia girls were "uppity." She talked, she preached, she scolded; and because she was one of their own, some of the farmers took her advice and began scraping up money to send their daughters to the school for an education. More than one of these families sat in the audience now, loudly applauding as Mary McLeod stood up to give her oration.

A week after the close of school, Mary was at the railroad station to get the train for Chicago. She was a very different looking person from the homely, bareheaded country girl who had stepped off the train seven years earlier. She wore the white shirtwaist she had made for graduation. Her long blue skirt was held trimly at the waist by a ribbon belt. She wore high, laced shoes, and a white-straw sailor hat was set on top of her pompadour. Miss Rebecca Cantcy had given her the hat and a pair of white gloves because, she said, that was the way people dressed in a big city.

Miss Cantcy and Miss Chapman had come to the station to see Mary off. So had Miss Cantcy's little sister, Cecilia, who insisted on carrying Mary's new brown-cardboard valise.

The train roared in and lurched to a stop. Mary took the valise, gave Cecilia a hurried embrace, and started to board the nearest car.

"Where the hell do you think you're going?" the conductor shouted.

Mary hesitated, one foot on the step.

"I mean you, there!" The voice was closer now. "You can't get on that coach. Colored coach is way up front by the engine. And you'd better hump it. Train ain't going to wait all day for you niggers!"

Jim Crow ... in her excitement Mary had forgotten. The day was gone when the red-plush luxury of the daycoaches was for anybody who had a ticket.

The car reserved for colored passengers was crowded. The seats were wooden. The floor was unswept. The windows were black with soot. It had formerly been the baggage car, and behind a low partition, half of it was still used for baggage—for boxes and trunks and for a lonesome whining dog. This was Mary's introduction to "Jim Crow" travel.

There had, of course, been much talk in the last few years at Scotia about this newest plan in the South to keep the Negro "in his place." The laws separating Negro and white passengers on the railroads and in other public places had started in Mississippi back in the seventies. They had spread like a contagious disease to Alabama, Louisiana, Florida, and Georgia. North Carolina and Virginia had finally caught the fever and so had the city of Washington, the National Capital, where Abraham Lincoln had lived and died.

Mary looked at the dirty floor, the unwashed windows. She heard the dog in the baggage section ahead yelping miserably. And for a moment she gave way to anger and despair. Had she learned to read just so she could read White and Colored signs in railroad stations? It didn't make sense.

With this thought some of her anger left her. Jim Crow couldn't last, because it wasn't sensible. And at least the whole South hadn't succumbed to the madness. In South Carolina you could still travel without being humiliated and made to feel like a piece of baggage. Mary remembered an editorial Miss Wilson had clipped from a South Carolina newspaper and sent to Dr. Satterfield. He had read it aloud at the dinner table.

> If there must be Jim Crow cars on the railroads, there should be Jim Crow on the street cars. If there are to be Jim Crow cars, there should be Jim Crow eating places . . . Jim Crow windows at tax offices where colored taxpayers pay for the privileges and blessings of citizenship . . . Jim Crow jury boxes in the courts and a Jim Crow Bible for colored witnesses to kiss.

The white editor in the South Carolina paper had showed just how crazy the new law was and where it would lead to. Mary felt comforted somehow and smiled at the woman next to her. She didn't dream that every absurdity that the newspaperman had thought up would be written into law—even to a separate Bible in the courtroom.

At Washington Mary changed trains. There was no separate car for Negroes on the train going on to Chicago. She sat up through the night on plush seats in a comfortable coach. But even so, and much as she loved traveling, much as she had looked forward to seeing more of America, she could take no pleasure in the journey. The ride on the converted baggage car stayed bitterly in her mind.

A Jim Crow car was a little thing compared to the deep injuries the Negro people had met with in their long sojourn in America. It was a little thing compared to the hardships Mary herself had met and overcome. But it was a step backward on the road to becoming free as other Americans are free. And a law was hard to fight.

Almost fifty years later, Mary was still fighting Jim Crow. She wrote:

> We must challenge, skillfully but resolutely, every sign of restriction or limitation on our full American citizenship. When I say challenge, I mean we must seek every opportunity to place the burden of responsibility on those who deserve it. If we simply accept and acquiesce in the face of discrimination, we accept the responsibility ourselves and allow those responsible to salve their conscience by believing that they have our acceptance and concurrence. We should, therefore, protest openly. . . . We must take the seat that our ticket calls for. . . . We must challenge everywhere the principle and practice of enforced racial segregation. Whenever one has the price or can fill the requirements for any privilege which is open to the entire public, that privilege must not be restricted on account of race.

Leadership in the struggle against Jim Crow was the end result—the fruit—of Mary's journey from Scotia, of her first direct experience with Jim Crow laws. The immediate result was only a dampening of her spirit so that some of the sparkle had gone out of her as she climbed wearily off the train in Chicago.

Chicago, in 1895, was just a half-century old. It was the city in all America that fired the imagination of Negroes in the rural South. What Philadelphia was in the days when slaves were seeking freedom through the Underground Railway, what Boston was to the Negro scholars who found at Harvard

University and at the homes of Wendell Phillips, Lloyd Garrison, Emerson, and the Alcotts a genuine welcome in the first years of Emancipation, what New York was to become in the eyes of Negroes of the 1920's, Chicago was at the time Mary McLeod first saw it. The bigness, the steel tracks converging from south and north and east and west to this one bundle of houses on the lake front, the drum of horses' hoofs, the hum and clatter of streetcars with straphangers of every age and race and condition, the foghorns in the harbor and the black ships on the blue water of the lake, the shouts of workmen handling bricks and steel high above the ground, the stockyards, the mills and factories, the libraries and schools, open to all people, the stone houses on the lake front with iron deer in the yards and pointed iron fences around the green, clipped lawns, the statues of Lincoln in the park, the gray slums with children jumping rope on the sidewalk, the sights, the smells, the noise, the laughter, all these Chicago offered to the incoming thousands.

To Mary McLeod, however, Chicago was just the place where the Moody Bible Institute held its classes, just the final stage in her training before the Presbyterian Board of Missions would send her across the ocean to bring the work of God to her kin in Africa.

When she stepped off the train, a group of men and women came up to her. They were fellow students from the Institute.

"How did you know me?"

Mary asked the same question she had asked long ago of Rebecca Cantcy. As then, she got no direct answer. The missionaries didn't like to say that she was different from the other colored passengers who got off the train, even though the difference now was that she was better dressed, more poised, more self-confident than the others—and had a blacker skin than most. Dr. Satterfield, writing to recommend Mary to Dr. Moody, had carefully mentioned her color.

Mary was the only Negro at the Institute. There were several students from India, and one or two from China, but her roommate was white. Her teachers were white, too. In a city teeming with people of African ancestry there was no contact and no sense of kinship between the men and women preparing to spend their lives converting Africans and the Negroes living in the next street or walking along the sidewalk whistling a tune whose rhythms were borrowed from African drums.

The Institute was in a somewhat dreary, gray, four-story building. It was both home and school to the students. Except for going out for field work—delivering tracts from house to house, singing, preaching in the prisons or almshouses—the students lived in a closed little world of their own.

Yet it was a remarkable world. Dwight Moody, the founder of the Institute, was an inspiring teacher, world-famous for his eloquence as an orator, and in addition, a vigorous and dedicated Bible scholar.

"Studying," he said, "goes deeper than mere reading. There are surface nuggets to be gathered but the best of the gold is underneath, and it takes time and labor to secure it."

Mary recognized in Dr. Moody a great soul and a thinker. She gave herself wholeheartedly to his leadership. She worked hard at her studies. Though she was, perhaps, a little lonely, she was filled with a sense of accomplishment. Miss Crissman would be satisfied, Mary hoped, because she was on the way to making good.

Then, at the end of the two years, the blow fell. The other men and women in training at the Institute were given posts at foreign missions. Their passage was arranged for. They packed their drab blue uniforms and their Bibles and prayer books.

But Mary was not given an appointment. The Board of Missions informed her gently, all kindness. They gave no reasons—just that it did not seem best to send her to Africa just now; later, perhaps, but the decision had been made. It was final.

Outwardly, Mary accepted the decision humbly and quietly. If to be a servant of God, to bring the words of gentle Jesus to her brothers and sisters across the seas was denied her, there must be a reason. She could not believe, if she was to keep her faith, that there was prejudice against a Negro missionary in the Church. In the Christian Church, Dr. Moody had said again and again, there is neither black nor white, rich nor poor, bond nor free. All stand equal before the face of the Master.

Therefore, Mary felt, the fault must be in herself. She would have to tell her parents. She would have to tell Miss Mary Crissman, and Miss Wilson, and the teachers at Scotia who had been so proud to recommend her because there were not many colored missionaries in the field. She would not have, to tell Granny, because Granny was dead. Telling Granny somehow would have been easy. The magnificent old woman would have had some words that would lift the weight from her heart.

Mary packed and went home—coach to Washington, then Jim Crow down to Mayesville. The South Carolina Legislature had given in at last. Mary read the White and Colored signs over the two doors of the Mayesville waiting-room. There had been only one door that time all the neighbors had come to see her off to Scotia. Suddenly it struck Mary as bitterly amusing. Jim Crow was costing the railroad money—all across the country they must have laid out money for those second doors.

Jim Crow had made another difference, Mary noticed, as she walked down the road toward her home. Two of her parents' white neighbors—the ones she used to help with their figuring— were lounging in front of the crossroads store when she passed. Not thinking of anything but a warm pleasure at seeing familiar faces, she called out a greeting. There wasn't any answer, just a stony stare.

With a jolt of understanding Mary glanced at the hand she had waved in friendliness. She jerked off the white gloves she had gotten accustomed to wearing in Chicago and looked at her black, blunt fingers. The years in schools and libraries had softened the callouses, but they were strong hands. They could still chop weeds and pick cotton.

The dignity of labor—that's what Mr. Booker T. Washington was always preaching. He was right, of course. But that speech he'd made in Atlanta was a mistake. He'd seemed to forget that labor couldn't have any dignity unless the laborer was accorded dignity, too.

Sally was home visiting with her week-old baby when Mary got there. Having Sally there somehow made it easier to tell about not getting the appointment. Her older sister's response was so typical it seemed like old times.

"Never did see any sense to going to Africa. Thing to do is get a cook job. Here you are twenty-two years old. When I was twenty-two—"

"You leave Mary alone," their mother broke in, just as always. "Mary's different. If God didn't want her to be a missionary, it's because He has other plans for her. Someday you'll see."

"*You've* got the somedays now, Mama," Mary laughed. Patsy's faith warmed her like pine knots crackling on a cold day. Maybe it was true about God needing her for other work. Maybe there was more than one way of being a servant of God.

Three months later Mary was on her knees, scrubbing the floor of the schoolhouse. Cotton was all picked. It was time for school to begin and it turned out that the term had been shortened to just two months a year.

Sam wasn't surprised when the plantation owners quietly put the pressure on to shorten the term of the mission school. They didn't want the children of sharecropper families wasting time on books.

Mary didn't waste any time doing something about that. She went from house to house wherever there were Negro children and told them to be in school on Monday, the first of November. She looked over the dogeared schoolbooks and slates Emma Wilson had stored away, and sat down and wrote to Scotia to send more books. And anything else they could think of, or spare.

Then she swept and scrubbed the schoolroom and cut a cord or so of wood for the big iron stove.

On the day school was to begin she dressed herself in her best white shirtwaist and dark-blue skirt and pinned a bangle to her collar because children like to see pretty things on their teacher. She walked the three miles to the church so fast that Hattie and little Margaret could barely keep up with her.

Hattie was almost thirteen. She had been to school off and on for several years. Mary had it in her mind to send her to Scotia someday. But Margaret was coming to school for the first time. Mary'd had to promise her a quarter for the circus next month to get her to come at all. And she didn't know where she'd get the quarter but she felt sure that the Lord would provide.

There were about twenty children playing in the yard waiting for school to begin. Mary stood in the doorway and looked them over. There were all ages, from about five years to a tall, well-dressed girl of fourteen. Most were barefoot, in patched threadbare dresses or overalls.

Which ones could read? Which needed special help? Were there any among them with the spark? Any with the kind of hunger for education that opens vistas ahead? Any who would "make good"?

Questions like these come to the mind of every born teacher on the first day of a new term of school. And Mary, from this moment to the end of her life, was such a teacher.

Serene, self-confident, she reached up to pull the bell rope.

"Good morning, children. My name is Miss McLeod."

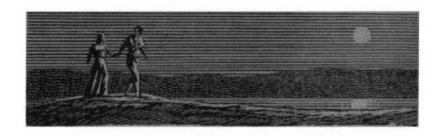

8. "The Bootstraps Must Be Strong"

OPENING SCHOOL that autumn and keeping it going until Miss Wilson arrived was a happy experience for Mary. She never doubted from the first week that teaching was meant to be her life work.

Still, the school at Mayesville was Miss Wilson's. There was need enough in Sumter County for a dozen teachers but not money enough for one. At Christmas time Mary wrote to the Board of Missions to ask if there was an opening in any one of the schools to which they gave support. She received a prompt answer suggesting that she apply to Haines Institute in Augusta, Georgia. Before the month was out she had a letter from Miss Lucy Laney offering her an immediate position.

Mary could not have found a better place to begin her teaching career. Haines Institute was already recognized as one of the best schools for colored boys and girls in the South. Its founder, Lucy Laney, was born a slave. Her father had been a carpenter on a large plantation near Mayesville. Sam and Patsy McLeod had heard of him because he had been a preacher as well as a carpenter. And he had bought his freedom. Ministers were rare in Sumter County in the 1850's. A slave who was permitted to earn enough to buy himself from his master was rarer still. Patsy recognized the name as soon as Mary got the letter from Augusta. She remembered Reverend Laney.

Carpentering and preaching, he had gone to Macon, Georgia. There he had married a slave girl owned by a family named Campbell. At once he had set himself the task of earning enough to buy his wife's freedom. It took a long time, and by the time his wife's freedom was purchased, they had two girl children, Annie and Lucy. He bought those children, too. His wife continued to work for the Campbells until after Emancipation. During that time Mrs. Campbell did a kind and generous thing. Quietly she defied the law against teaching Negroes. She taught little Lucy to read and write.

While her mother dusted and swept the library, the child was allowed to go in and read the books. David and Louise Laney had eight more children. They managed to give all ten of them a little schooling. During the Reconstruction period an elementary school was opened in Macon. First Lucy, and after her each of the children, was sent to school. Lucy went on to a normal school just opened in Atlanta. This was the school which later became the kernel, the core of Atlanta University. It was an inspired institution, founded in the flush of hope and confidence of the Reconstruction. Lucy Laney graduated with the first class. They were a dedicated group of young men and women, feeling themselves destined through the grace of God to spread the gift of reading to the freedmen. Education was too hard to come by, too precious a thing to keep just for your own pleasure.

Lucy went home to teach in Macon, then in the little town of Conyers, and later in Savannah.

The schools were all in makeshift buildings—in a church, in a made-over barn, in a log cabin. All the children, from the youngest to the oldest, were in one room. The salaries of the teachers ranged from $12.50 to $18.00 a month. None of the schools gave instruction beyond the seventh grade.

Schools like these, scattered over the South, had reduced illiteracy from 90 per cent at the time of Emancipation to 60 per cent in 1886. Almost half of the freedmen and the children of freedmen had somehow been taught to read and write and figure—a little. For Lucy Laney, that wasn't good enough. There was more that her people stood in need of: A knowledge of history, of music and painting and literature—the things she had learned to prize as a child, studying in Mrs. Campbell's library—were still denied to colored children in the South. And they needed to know the history of their own people, to learn both family pride and race pride. All of these things Lucy Laney was convinced must be given the children in order that they might have the benefits of free Americans.

There were colleges Negroes could attend—Howard, in the nation's capital; Oberlin, Wilberforce, and Lincoln in the North, Fisk University in Tennessee. But the young people in the South had no way to prepare to enter college.

Schools like the Hampton Industrial Institute in Virginia and the newly formed school at Tuskegee, Alabama, provided learning somewhat beyond the elementary level, it was true, but they did not have the purpose of preparing their students for college training. On the contrary, Hampton Institute's prospectus announced firmly that "no classics are taught," and Booker T. Washington at Tuskegee wanted to be careful "not to educate our students out of sympathy with agricultural life, so that they would be attracted from the country to the cities, and yield to the temptation of trying to live by their wits."

In the deep South, in 1886, there was not one public high school a Negro pupil could attend. And there was little hope that money for high schools would be provided. The bright days of Reconstruction were over. The public school systems founded by Negroes and whites sitting in legislative halls together had continued and improved—for the white population. For every dollar spent on public education, ninety-three cents went to white schools, seven cents to the education of Negroes. The excuse was poverty and the burden of rebuilding a land ravaged by war. But it was not poverty alone that kept the Southern legislators of the post-Reconstruction period from giving adequate education to a people longing for education. If that had been so, they would have welcomed help from the rest of the nation. Instead, white teachers from the North who came to teach in the mission schools were ostracized and insulted. The number of hardy spirits willing to brave this treatment was decreasing.

"If our people are going to be raised up, it will be by their own bootstraps," Lucy Laney argued. "And the bootstraps had better be strong!"

Lucy Laney wrote to the Presbyterian Board of Missions to ask for help in founding a school—one that would meet the standards of a high school, housed in a building with separate classrooms, with a meeting-hall, with living-quarters for students and teachers.

They answered, giving their warm encouragement to the idea of such a school, but no financial support. After all, the members of the Board had never heard of a young woman by the name of Lucy Laney. Dozens of requests for funds came to them every month, and there was at the moment far more interest in sending missionaries to Africa than in spending money in the South.

Miss Laney was disappointed, but she did not give up. "Africans in America need Christ and schooling just as much as Negroes in Africa," she declared.

With the encouragement of her father and a hundred dollars contributed by the Ladies Aid Society of his church, she went to the town of Augusta, Georgia, where there were no schools for colored children at all. She rented a ramshackle cottage and opened The Haines Normal and Industrial Institute.

It was a long name for a school with one teacher and five students. Over the years, however, the Presbyterian Board of Missions was able to give the school financial help as well as sponsorship, and when Mary McLeod came to teach ten years later, Miss Laney had a three-story building and several cottages. She had more than a hundred students and fifteen teachers. And on her wall was a picture of a four-story brick building she meant to build next year, if the Lord was willing.

The school was right in town, surrounded by the miserable unpainted houses of the colored poor. It wasn't beautiful, as Scotia had been. But it was a well-ordered school, with more books in the library than Mary had ever seen. The history and literature classes were as rich and stimulating as could be found in many women's colleges in the East. The very best artists available were brought to the school in order that the pupils might know and love those things that were best in all the arts. Negro History was one of the "musts" for high school students. And from the kindergarten classes through high school, Lucy Laney trained her pupils in singing.

It was in the music especially that Mary reveled. She had loved the music at Scotia, but here the blending of boys' voices with the girls' was even more beautiful. Miss Laney's alto voice was an inspiration as she trained the choir to sing the beloved hymns. And as the students learned to sing, they became aware of the place that the spirituals had in the history of their people—how the spirituals, born in the bitterness of slavery and tuned to the music of Africa, were the freedom songs of the enslaved people. "My name is called and I must go, . . . I heard from Heaven today," the choir sang; and they knew as they sang that, not very many years before, those very words had been sung by some slave, somewhere in the South, to say good-by to his fellow captives before he made his break for freedom. "My Lord, what a morning—when the stars begin to fall. . . . "The dream of freedom, the faith that God would not let the winter of their captivity last forever—and in the days of the Underground Railroad, the very practical instructions to slaves following the North Star—all these were embodied in the hymns of slavery times.

Without realizing at all the full meaning of the spirituals, white Americans all over the South—all over the country, in fact—had been stirred by the music of the Hampton Choir, the Fisk Jubilee Singers. And wealthy people were moved to make desperately needed contributions toward the schools for the colored. Contributions meant more teachers, more books, more scholarships.

A good part of the support of Haines Institute came from singing. Augusta was a winter resort, a popular place for wealthy Northerners to come to escape the cold and snows. Lucy Laney had spared no effort to interest these visitors in her school. It was not easy to dramatize the quiet scholarly work in the classrooms. But the spirituals could be used to attract visitors to the school who might be impelled to contribute. Never a carriage was seen driving up to the door but the signal would go out from Miss Laney's office. Quick as a fire drill, the neatly uniformed students would line up in the halls to march to the chapel for an impromptu concert. These concerts brought in dollars for library books or for the building fund. They made it possible for the children of Baptist and Methodist and Presbyterian ministers to come to school free, because Miss Laney knew just how small a minister's salary was. They had brought philanthropists who served on the Board of Trustees.

Sometimes it was a little annoying, if Mary was in the midst of explaining an algebra problem when the buzzer sounded, to have the class stand up and march out of the room. But she understood the terrible need for money if you didn't have any. If a song could reach the pocketbooks of the wealthy, then they'd better sing. God would understand.

When she got a school of her own, Mary decided, she'd fill it with song—not just for attracting the attention of people who could give money, but as an outlet for all the longings of her people.

For Mary McLeod had the "somedays" again. Her whole mind was bent on the day her own school would become a reality.

That it would be a reality, she didn't doubt. It would look like Scotia, with all the beauty she could put into it. It would train boys and girls to work for a living—all sorts of skilled trades and farming would be taught, the way Hampton Institute and now Tuskegee were doing. But the teaching would be like Miss Laney's, too—giving of the world's learning to all her pupils, preparing those who had the special ability and desire for further, higher studies.

"Vocational training," she wrote later, "includes not only the technique of actual work, but intelligent comprehension of duties as a citizen and the ability to partake of the higher spiritual life of this world."

Her school must also be a living part of the community. It would stir up people to do something about the Jim Crow laws and about the lynchings. It would keep men voting even if they risked their lives to do it. It would be a rallying place for citizenship of the fathers— and yes, for the mothers, too. Negro women, thank Heaven, didn't need to be reminded that they had human responsibilities; they did need guidance, though, and her school would give it. But mainly there would be the children—she dreamed at night of "big brick buildings and little children."

At twenty-four, Mary McLeod knew what kind of school she wanted. She had the belief in herself that was necessary for the work. But she didn't have an idea in the world how to go about getting a school.

Yet Lucy Laney had done it. Booker T. Washington had done it. Miss Nannie Burroughs had done it. You had to find philanthropists, you had to find trustees, you had to find pupils. She couldn't find any of these while teaching at Haines Institute. But she could prepare herself. She could learn from Miss Laney, from the books in the library, and from the visitors who came to Haines.

Dr. Madison C. B. Mason was one of those who came. Young, highly educated, well dressed, easy of manner, he was the first Negro to be made head of the Methodist Freedmen's Aid and Southern Education Society. It was his job to raise money for schools in the South and to recommend schools that should be supported. He was a great admirer of Lucy Laney. Mary listened to their talk at the supper table, hungrier for knowledge than for the clabber and cold meat and spoonbread. Dr. Mason thought the time had come to consolidate. There were, he said, too many small, private, inefficient schools begging for money. Perhaps the time for those had passed. A few fine schools like Haines— when Miss Laney got her new brick building on Gwinnett Street—could be an example.

"If any of my daughters want to teach when they grow up," he said, "I'd send them to Haines to learn how."

Mary's hope sank. If Dr. Mason thought there were already too many small private schools he wouldn't want to help her start another. He couldn't know hers wouldn't be inefficient.

Mary wondered, though. How many children throughout the South could manage to attend a few large schools? Had Dr. Mason forgotten about the million children on the plantations and at little crossroads towns who didn't even have the benefit of one-room cabin schools? Had he looked around him on the way from the railroad station at the boys and girls running loose in back alleys? For every hundred getting the fine education Miss Laney offered there must be a thousand right here in Augusta without any training at all.

However, Dr. Mason's discussion had given Mary an idea. Suppose she went to some school that was just rocking along, and was able to build it up. Suppose she I showed what she could do?

She stayed another year at Haines, until she heard of a school that was being opened in Sumter. It was near her home and might give her the opportunity she was looking for.

Miss Laney was sorry to see Mary go. Haines would never have a better mathematics teacher. And the school choir would be the poorer without Mary's deep contralto voice. But Lucy Laney understood sympathetically the younger woman's reasons.

Kendall Institute at Sumter was small. It was not nearly so good as Haines. Mary threw herself into building it up, but she was a little sorry she had left Haines Institute. She seemed no nearer getting a school of her own, and she missed Lucy Laney.

There was twenty years' difference in their ages and a vast difference in background and temperament. Lucy Laney was small, with wide-set melting eyes, sensitive mouth, and short-cropped curly hair. She was city bred and knew only by hearsay the toil that goes with wresting a living from the land. Yet the bond between them had been close—closer than Mary realized until she was away. She needed somebody to talk to.

One day a young man, a teacher at Kendall, asked if he could see Mary home from the Wednesday night song service. The school wasn't big enough to have much of a choir, so Mary had organized a singing society in the near-by church. She had to have music. It was the breath of life to her. The young teacher liked music, too. He knew a lot about music and he had a beautiful tenor voice that blended with her own contralto.

Alburtus Bethune had a way with him when he wanted to, and he soon got the habit of walking with her every Wednesday evening.

Mary found herself talking to him as she had never talked to a man before. When she told him about having tried to be a missionary he brought her books about African art. He listened by the hour to her theories of education, to her "someday" plans for a school. He brought her presents—a leather-bound volume of John Greenleaf Whittier's poetry, a box of chocolates, a fan from Japan.

When spring came and the azaleas were in bloom and the air was heavy with the sweetness of wild honeysuckle, he asked her to marry him.

Mary had had admirers before, but never a man of charm and education, never a teacher whose interest and goals seemed so like her own.

Together, they'd start a school that would send out a host of young people to right the wrongs that crowded in on their people. Mary wasn't afraid of marriage. She had grown up in a household rooted in love.

Mary McLeod and Alburtus Bethune were married in January 1900. Shortly afterward, Alburtus had an offer to teach in a church school in Savannah. "There'd be a place on the faculty for you, too," he said to Mary, looking up from the letter. "That is, if you want it"

"Of course I want it," she answered, a little puzzled. "What would I do if I weren't teaching?"

Alburtus laughed and put his arm around her. "Well I was thinking, in Savannah we'd find a house to live in and raise a family."

Naturally, Mary wanted a child, but that didn't mean she'd give up teaching. God intended that she should build a school. Surely Alburtus understood that.

"Oh sure, honey," her young husband agreed amiably.

It was settled, then. They'd go to Savannah to teach. He'd go ahead and find a place for them to live. She could spend a few days with her family in Mayesville.

Alburtus went home with her for a night and a day. Then he left and Mary was alone with her family. In midwinter, work was at a standstill. The younger girls were going to school—walking, as Mary had, the three miles there and back every day. Sam was chopping frees, clearing what was left of the swamp for a rice crop next year. Mary and Patsy had time in the house together. They didn't sit idle, of course, but there was fame for talk.

"Why is it, Mama, that it's the women of our race who seem to look farther ahead to what's needed?"

Patsy looked up from her ironing. "Farther than menfolk? Is that what you mean, daughter? Ain't that nature? A woman carry a child in the womb and Jesus say for her to think ahead for that child. 'Take no thought for your life, what ye shall eat or what ye shall drink, nor what raiment ye shall put on. Is not life more than meat and the body more than raiment?' He says. And you sit thinking of a world of goodness and love. You think of your children multiplied by the millions. God sharpens your eyes to the needs of the world."

Patsy carried the iron back to the stove with quick, firm steps. She was sixty-eight years old, now, but to Mary it seemed as if they were one age—friends puzzling out things together.

"But when the child is born you have to think of its meat and drink, the raiment it will wear," Mary said.

"So you go back to work by your man in the fields. But you don't close your eyes. You still see the vision."

"But the women of leisure, the white ladies, they bear children, too. Why can't they see, most of them?"

"They give over the care of their offspring," Patsy slapped the iron down. "And I don't just mean they hire nurses—them 'faithful old mammies' they always braggin' about. I mean they give over workin' for their offspring. White ladies ain't got a mumblin' word to say about what kind of world their children's goin' to live in. You take Mrs. Wilson, she got no say about her young. We have a hard life, but I wouldn't change with her. Seem like she's just half a person. Childbearing, working, tryin' to move the world forward a little bit—they all got to go together, daughter."

Mary was satisfied. Her mother had swept away the doubts Alburtus had raised. Having a child wouldn't keep her from doing the work God called her to do. Childbearing and work, they went together—if you were lucky enough to have a good man and were girded by a faith in the world. It was a good time to start a new life with all the things that needed to be done.

But the school in Savannah did not offer the opportunity Mary needed. It was pleasant enough; but just as Dr. Mason had said about some schools, it just rocked along. It had a meagre library and no science, no training for living in the new world of the twentieth century.

Alburtus seemed satisfied. Mary herself was restless. She was going to have a baby and for several months before the baby was to be born had given up teaching. She took long walks around Savannah, mainly down to the docks. Savannah gave her the ocean. The pound and the sweep and the rhythm, the limitless horizon lifted her like a new song. Mary McLeod Bethune and the ocean belonged together. When she and Alburtus got their school, she wanted it by the ocean.

After their son, little Albert, was born, she had more reason than ever for wanting to move to something new. There was an opening for both Alburtus and herself in a mission school in Palatka, Florida. The salary was no better than they had been getting in Savannah, but living would be cheaper in a small town. They might be able to save a little money. With a baby to care for, it wouldn't be easy to manage the teaching; but, remembering all the work her mother had done, with seventeen children underfoot, that was a problem Mary was confident of solving.

Rocking her son to sleep at night, Mary thought a lot about her mother and her grandmother and the burdens women had carried through the long years of slavery and afterward. The struggle had made them strong. All over the country their strength was carrying the race upward. But they were like separate threads. Bind the separate strands together in a rope and you'd have something! There ought to be some way to unite the strength of the colored women in the South. For one thing, they ought to be voting alongside their men. Frederick Douglass had seen that. And there were colored women working right along for suffrage in the North. Down here there wasn't any association of women. "The strength of a Lucy Laney building her school and the strength of Mama in the cotton field," Mary said to herself, "they ought to be knit together. Someday God will give me a chance to do something about that." But first, somehow, she had to get a school of her own.

9. Sweet-Potato Pies

THE BETHUNES had been at Palatka for two years, but Mary
had come no closer to her goal. Living in this little town on the
St. Johns River was cheaper than in a city. She'd hoped that they
would be able to save something every payday, to make a start
at getting a school. She had a name for it already—The Bethune
Industrial and Normal Institute.

Her husband agreed that it was a good plan to save, but he
liked nice things. He liked to buy presents for her and for the
little boy. He was satisfied with teaching at Palatka even if it
wasn't the best school in the world; he was satisfied with leading
the choir at church on Sunday and digging in the garden Mary
had planted and fishing in the St. Johns River or reading poetry
aloud under a live oak tree dripping with gray moss.

But it was 1904 and Mrs. Bethune was almost thirty years old
and she was tired of waiting. There was talk of big things stirring
on the east coast. Families from Alabama, from Georgia were

passing through Palatka, camping out overnight on the river bank with all their belongings piled up on wagons and the children sleeping on quilts spread under the wagons and the mules tethered to a near-by tree. In the morning they'd take the ferry across the river and disappear at the turn of the road going toward the rising sun.

Mrs. Bethune went down to the river bank and talked to some of the women. She always liked to talk to strangers.

"Where we headin' for? The railroad! A man come through where we was staying, said there's work to be had. Track-layin' and buildin' for a railroad all down along the ocean. Work that pay money wages. Cash money, spend it where you see fit."

"You've been sharecropping?" Mrs. Bethune knew how that was, having to get credit from the landlord, never seeing a cent when your cotton was sold, owing it all on last year's debts.

"Thought we never would get free of the plantation. And things are bad, real bad, back in Georgia. Go down to Florida, maybe things be better for bringin' up the children."

Most of the families were headed for Daytona. That was where the railroad yards were now.

What about churches? What about homes? What about schooling for the children? Mary asked questions that no one could answer. All they knew was that there was work for the menfolk—with wages. And Mr. Flagler, the man who was building the railroad, was putting up a fancy hotel. Northern people were coming down for the winter sunshine. Rich folks.

Likely there'd be cook jobs for the women, too. As for houses—most of them had never had anything better than a dirt-floor shack. And not more than one family out of three had come from a town with a school their children could attend.

When Dr. Mason came to Palatka a few months later on his regular inspection tour, Mary asked about the developments on the east coast. All those families going to Daytona—were their children to grow up in ignorance? And if it was true that Northern visitors were coming in for the winter as they had at Augusta, Georgia— couldn't they help support a school? It was people like that who had helped Lucy Laney build Haines Institute.

Dr. Mason agreed that, in time, Daytona might become a real winter resort—but that was years ahead. Conditions were pretty rough there now, he'd heard. He didn't consider the time was ripe for founding a school.

Meanwhile, Mary Bethune thought, there are those children going to live in shanties without any knowledge of books or decent living. Who was going to teach those children to read?

She talked to her husband about going to Daytona to open a school. She knew they had very little money saved. Not more than ten or fifteen dollars. But the Lord provided ways when his children gave the necessary push. With His help, they'd manage. Alburtus Bethune explained carefully that Mary's plan wasn't practical. Anyway, they didn't have ten dollars any more; there was just $1.50 left in their savings. He hadn't meant to let her know until her birthday, but he had sent to Atlanta for a very special birthday present for her.

Mary took the dollar and a half and packed a bag with her clothes and the little boy's. She tied up a few schoolbooks she had and fixed a package of food. Her mind was made up. She would start a school in Daytona. God would guide her every step of the way.

When she was settled, she would write Alburtus and he could come if he wished. And when he came, would he be sure to bring their bicycles? She spent the night straightening the two rooms of their cottage to leave everything neat and comfortable for him. In the morning, she went down to the river and begged a ride for herself and the little boy from one of the families traveling to Daytona.

The trip was a little more than seventy miles and took two nights and three days. Before she came in sight of the camp for the railroad workers, outside the little town, she had already got the promise of two young girls as pupils in the school she was going to open. And her dollar and a half was still intact. She remembered the name and address of an acquaintance in Daytona. Mrs. Walker would be willing to put her up for the night, she felt sure. She might even know some people who would help get the school started.

Mrs. Bethune walked through the colored section looking for the street number of her friend. Albert trudged along beside her and she walked slowly, shortening her stride so he could keep up.

"Here's the place, son. I was sure I could find it," she said at last.

Mrs. Walker welcomed them warmly. Company was always a pleasure. But after Albert was safely in bed, the Daytona woman listened without enthusiasm to plans for a school.

"There's a county school," she said, "for the few that want to send their children. The whites won't want another school. It'll just make trouble. You'll see. They'll be afraid if our girls get education they won't go out to do housework. And as for the railroad gangs, they don't mean those people to stay after the railroad is built. Anyhow, what in the world will you do for money?"

But Mary McLeod Bethune had her mind made up. Nothing was going to stop her. Next morning she took Albert by the hand and went down to the ocean front. That's where she wanted her school—within sight and sound of the sea.

While the little boy collected shells on the beach, Mary strode up and down the white, hard-packed sand and laid out a program for herself. It wasn't much like the plan she'd dreamed of. Faith Hall and a library, "gracious living" and trustees would have to come later. Right now she needed a roof over her head and some boxes and lumber and things for furniture. She needed a cookstove. And some piepans. For the sight of that drab and doleful work-camp at the railroad yards had given her an idea for raising money to get the school started.

There were a few shacks at the camp for families to live in, but the main part of the camp was made up of barracks that served as sleeping-quarters for single men. She didn't know how those men were fed, but she was sure they could use something special in the way of food.

Sweet potatoes were dirt cheap all over Florida and her sweet-potato pies were as good as anybody's and better than most. She would divide her days between teaching and making and selling sweet-potato pies! Baked yams, too, for those who couldn't afford a pie. She and her pupils could carry them, piping hot, in buckets, down to the railroad yards when the whistle blew for lunch.

Sweet potatoes—that would do it. God works in mysterious ways His wonders to perform.

"Come on, honey," she said to her son. "We've got to get busy. Nothing comes without faith and prayer. Nothing in my life has ever come without sweat, too."

Mary Bethune found an old unoccupied house on the edge of "colored town" where the peninsula narrowed and you could see a little of the ocean. There was nothing beyond it but a dump heap. The cottage had once been painted white or gray. Most of the paint had peeled off and the front steps sagged under her feet when she went up to stare through the window. But there were glass panes in the windows. The rooms looked large. Some straggly fig trees and palms outlined what had once been a garden. A gourd vine crawled over the porch railings. It was a better place than most of the shacks or log-cabin churches that housed the schools for colored children over the South.

Before the day was out, she had found the owner and cajoled him into renting the house to her for eleven dollars a month, to be paid as soon as she was able. From the white man's viewpoint this was not very sound business management. But he probably figured that it was good to have somebody living on his property, especially with all the strangers overrunning the town.

"You can live in the house—you and the little boy have to live somewhere, I reckon," he said. He warned her, though, that there "wasn't any use starting a nigger school." They already had one in the county.

"A mile or two up the road," he explained, "at the Colored Baptist Church. The church gives 'em the use of the building— such as it is—County pays the teachers—two of 'em—fifteen dollars a month out of *our* taxes! Gave 'em the old desks, too, when we built our new school. I hear they've got more than a hundred little darkies studying—up to the third grade. That's as far as the colored can learn, my pastor said."

Mrs. Bethune thought of graduation day at Scotia. She thought of Mary Church Terrell who graduated from Oberlin College and knew seven languages better than this man knew one. She thought of Dr. W. E. B. DuBois at Atlanta University, who had a Ph.D. from Harvard and had studied in Berlin, Germany. She thought of the hundreds of other college teachers. She thought of Paul Dunbar and James Weldon Johnson, whose poems were printed in the best magazines in the country.

Mary Bethune said: "Thank you, sir"; and paid fifty cents down on the rent. She had more important things to do than to start educating this ignorant white man. She put the key he gave her in her pocket.

One hurdle was over. She had a roof over her head! And being close to the town dump had its advantages. She would be likely to find some good lumber for making furniture and, if God was willing, maybe a cast-off cookstove.

She picked Albert up in her arms, because he was looking a little tired, and carried him down the newly laid railroad tracks until she came to the camp for the track-layers.

She hunted up the families of the two girls she had enrolled as pupils and while she went from door to door inquiring for the newcomers she picked up three more pupils. One girl had gone through the second grade in Atlanta. The other two had never lived where there was a school. They would have to begin from the beginning—as she had, at the age of eleven.

It was dinner time and she ate with one of the families and fed Albert and let him run around a little and play with the swarm of children.

The pupils who were coming with her to live at the schoolhouse were told to bring their own pallets to sleep on and what clothes they had.

"We'll have uniforms, later, blue for everyday and white for Sunday," she explained with superb confidence. "And real beds to sleep on—a separate bed for each of you—and a bureau and writing table. Pictures on the wall and curtains at the windows."

The mother of one of the students offered to hitch up the mule and drive Mrs. Bethune and the children back to the house. She accepted gratefully. On the way out to the field where the mule was tethered, she saw two big packing-boxes.

"If those don't belong to anybody," she said, "I'll just adopt them. I read an article recently in an anthropological journal. It was about a primitive Indian tribe in California. They lived by gathering the wild resources of the land. They grew nothing, bought nothing. Gatherers is what we'll have to be to get my Industrial and Normal Training Institute started!"

There were some things that even a person of Mary Bethune's ingenuity would have to buy. On the way to Mrs. Walker's to get her valise and the package of books, she stopped at the general store and bought six pieplates to make sweet-potato pies and a second-hand iron pot for general cooking, a few forks and a knife, and a scrubbing brush. Her money gave out before she got any food. She'd have to borrow some corn meal and lard from Mrs. Walker. And a hammer . . .

"Wrap every item separately, please," she said to the storekeeper. Good, clean wrapping paper would give the girls something to write on for the first week at least. Mary had already spied out a bush of elderberries growing near the house. Boiled down, the juice would do nicely for ink. There were sure to be some barnyard fowls in the neighborhood where she could help herself to feather quills for pens. Or she could burn wood down to charcoal for pencils. She didn't see any way to get a blackboard and chalk yet—but the Lord would provide.

When they had left the Walkers' and started down the shabby, dusty street toward the house by the dump heap, Mary Bethune began to sing.

She couldn't help herself—the fullness of her gratitude to God for giving her a school had to be expressed. She missed her husband's melodious voice.

"Alburtus has a beautiful tenor voice," she said to herself, "but he's just not serious about education."

10. "In My Mind, in My Spirit"

WITH HER OWN little son, her five pupils, and the mother of one of them watching, Mary Bethune turned the key in the door of her schoolhouse. But before she pushed the door inward on its rusty hinges, she said a little prayer. "We thank thee, Lord, for this school building. Let these girls enter to learn; let them depart to serve. We ask it in the name of gentle Jesus. Amen."

"Enter to learn; depart to serve." Someday the words would be cut into the stone portal of her school; until then, they were many times on her lips. To learn and to serve—these were Mary McLeod Bethune's watchwords. She opened the door and strode through the hall. There were four rooms and a loft in the house, and a back porch with two boards missing from the floor. The walls were hung with spider-webs, the air was musty, and a rat scurried across the floor and down a gaping hole in the baseboard of the front room. But there was a fireplace and glass windows in all but one room and a rocking-chair with just one arm gone stood near the hearth. And a sulfur well in the cellar. It was the best house the five little girls had ever seen.

Mrs. Bethune tugged at the windows until they were opened wide and the fresh, salt air of the ocean swept through. From the back porch they could see the water stretching out to the horizon. Tall grass and scrubby trees and bushes were all that lay between their back yard and the white shining beach.

The girls wanted to start unloading the wagon, bring in their pallets, and choose their sleeping room. Mrs. Bethune said unloading was a good idea so Mrs. Jones could get home to her family, but the only thing they could bring up for the present was the scrubbing brush—the house had to be spanking clean before anything could go into it.

"You need a broom for these cobwebs, Mrs. Bethune," the oldest girl said at once. "I'll fetch some twigs and a stout stick to make a broom."

Before dark, the house was scrubbed and cleaned, and a fire was laid in the fireplace for cooking hoecake for supper. Mrs. Bethune left the girls laying out their pallets and covers, the three youngest in one room, the two oldest in another. She took the quilt off the package of books and tucked Albert into it. He had been asleep for an hour curled up in the broken rocking-chair.

She laid the books out on one of the packing cases; a Bible, Maury's *Geography*, her old blue-back speller, the leather-bound volume of John Greenleaf Whittier's poetry her husband had given her when they were courting. These, with the Fisk Jubilee songbook, and the algebra from which she had taught at Haines, were her library.

But someday books would line the walls of a redbrick school building. She could see it clearly in her mind's eye as she walked up the road to find a house where she could beg a bucket of milk for the children's supper.

Mary Bethune never considered begging beneath her dignity. Anything that was needed, she could ask for in such a way people felt she was doing a favor to permit them to contribute. She didn't hesitate now to walk up to the kitchen door of a house at the other end of Oak Street, swinging the wooden bucket from her well. There was a barn in back of the cottage, so most likely the people kept a cow.

A sallow-skinned old lady in a Mother Hubbard dress came out on the porch.

"Fixing to open a school for colored girls!" she snapped, when Mary Bethune had explained her errand. "Well, I don't hold with educating darkies—just makes 'em discontented—but I see you know your place, coming to the back door and all. And I don't see no use letting children, white or black, go hungry while I've got more buttermilk than my pig can use. I churn butter for the people building Mr. Flagler's new hotel and the buttermilk piles up. You can send one of the girls over every day and get some—I'm right glad somebody's coming to live in that tumbledown old house." All the while she was talking the old lady was ladling buttermilk into the bucket. "I saw the wagon turn into Oak Street," the old lady said. "But I didn't see no furniture."

Mrs. Bethune thought it just as well to answer honestly that she didn't have any furniture yet, but the Lord had appointed her to start this school; she had faith that He would provide— the faith of the Twenty-third Psalm.

The bucket was full, but the old lady let it sit on the table. Her eyes narrowed cautiously and she stared at Mrs. Bethune's black skin, shining with sweat.

"You can read the Bible? Sure enough read the words, I mean?" The white woman's gnarled hand fumbled in her dress pocket. "Because if you can, maybe you can read a letter for me—from my son. I just don't happen to know where my spectacles are."

The steel-rimmed spectacles were in plain sight on the kitchen shelf but Mary McLeod Bethune understood. No white person, however ignorant, could admit that he knew less than a Negro, however many college degrees the Negro had—not in the Southern states of the United States—not in the year 1904.

She read the short, poorly written communication in a level, expressionless voice. It was from Chicago. The son was well, didn't have a job yet but expected to be hired soon if some stinking black boy didn't step up and get the job he was after.

As Mrs. Bethune walked down the steps with the brimming pail of buttermilk, the old lady blurted out: "I don't know as you want it—but there's a old cookstove out in the shed. It's not doing me any good."

Mary's luck held day after day, though she never believed in luck. Victory through faith was her way of putting it.

A farmer riding toward town with a wagon full of produce agreed to sell, on credit, the sweet potatoes and eggs she needed for making her pies. On Sunday she took the girls to the nearest Negro church, not caring about its denomination since there were among her pupils Methodists and Baptists and one Presbyterian, like herself. The pastor announced the coming of the new school to Daytona. Several women came up to her afterward to say they had things they could spare. One had a chair. Another had a frying pan. A third, a real nice square of matting for a carpet. Next evening after dark, one of the deacons of the congregation brought Mrs. Bethune a big washtub full of dishes. He explained that he worked as a butler in the banker's family. His mistress had bought a new set of dishes and said he could have these if he wanted them. Mrs. Bethune didn't know whether she was happier to have the beautiful china dishes or the washtub they came in!

With the first money that came from selling pies, she bought a sadiron. She had already made some soap with lye and wood ashes. Now they could wash and iron their clothes properly. Bathing was no problem, with the whole ocean less than a quarter of a mile away. But a washtub meant hot water and snowy, boiled clothes hanging on the line.

As Mrs. Bethune had anticipated, the dumping ground provided boxes to sit on, boards for shelves to hold books, a new arm for the rocker, and all sorts of small treasures, such as a cracked mirror so the girls could see that their hair was neat and trim. The great liveoaks that grew on the lot were hung with Spanish moss. Mrs. Bethune gathered it to stuff ticking for pallets for herself and little Albert. The well had no cover. A piece of old iron from the dump made a safe covering. One of the girls found a couple of small wheels that could go on a wagon. Albert would have something to play with, and even a two-wheeled wagon would be useful for hauling.

Mrs. Bethune kept to her plan of having lessons half the day and devoting the other hours to making and selling pies to the railroad workers. Prayers and reading from the Bible morning and evening and singing the songs from the Fisk Jubilee songbook gave a pattern, a unity to the day.

A few more girls enrolled in the school as day scholars. They were from Daytona families and had gone as far as they could in the county school. Their parents worked mostly as domestics in the big houses and were able to pay a dollar a month for the girls' instruction. The families of her boarding scholars paid, too, when they could. And one morning when everybody was getting pretty tired of a diet of cornbread, buttermilk, and wild berries, she found a big box of groceries on her doorstep, brought by some of the railroad men to whom she sold her sweet-potato pies.

Then, the first of the new year, when Flagler's handsome hotel was finished, winter tourists started coming to Daytona Beach. Mary Bethune had been waiting for this moment. In her crisp white shirtwaist and skirt, she carried a basket of pies to peddle to the wealthy vacationers. To each customer she explained that they were made by the pupils of the Daytona Educational and Industrial Training School. The pies served as introduction to tell about her school.

Several thoughtful men and women, wintering at the fabulous new resort of Mr. Flagler, began to look forward to the brief exchange with this witty, intelligent colored woman who took her stand two or three afternoons a week outside the landscaped grounds.

There was, in the early years of the new century, a revival of interest outside the South in the condition of the Southern Negro. For a long time, Booker T. Washington had successfully appealed to a few upper-class whites in Southern states and to Northern industrialists to support vocational schools for Negroes. The money for Tuskegee in Alabama, for Hampton in Virginia, and for a dozen smaller schools came from these groups. They accepted the idea that a little education for the Negro was, on the whole, a good thing—with the understanding that "the race was not amenable to the intellectual regime applicable to whites" and that humility and service would be taught along with the rudiments of learning. To contribute to a manual-training school in a Southern state had become a comfortable, a respectable philanthropy.

Mary Bethune knew very well that this was not enough, would never be enough to guarantee full equality and the unalienable rights of citizenship! But it was progress from the bleak years when the Negro had to depend entirely on his own efforts or on the efforts of a few church missionary societies. Mrs. Bethune's goals went far beyond the limited program of those who were content to train the Negro man to be forever a laborer and the Negro woman to play the role of a domestic servant. But money to support a school had to come from somewhere. She saw these vacationers from the North as a source of help and she used every means she could to interest them in her school.

One man in particular became a steady customer for her pies. He was James N. Gamble and he was a manufacturer of soap. Mrs. Bethune talked to him several times about the needs of the colored people and about her school and sensed his sympathy and interest. She remembered the importance Lucy Laney had placed on having white trustees of Haines Institute. She talked about the buildings she meant to have. The red-brick hall and chapel—Faith Hall—was as vivid to her as if it already stood on the field overlooking the ocean. She talked about the science laboratory and the library; about the neatly uniformed scholars living in comfort and decency while they learned to study; about the place her school was to have in the community.

Because this rather somber man in the high, stiff collar and black tie listened so intently and with such apparent good will, Mrs. Bethune felt emboldened one day, toward the end of the season, to ask him to become a trustee of the Daytona Educational and Industrial Training School.

He didn't say he would, but he didn't say he wouldn't, either. She invited him to call at the school any time. Mrs. Bethune sold the rest of her pies and walked back to her unpainted house on the edge of the dump heap, well pleased with the day's accomplishment.

A few mornings later she was working outside the little shed she had rigged up as a kitchen. The black kettle was full of steaming sweet potatoes which some of the girls were peeling and mashing. Others were rolling the dough for the pie crust. All were working on the day's pies except the oldest girl, who was reading aloud from Maury's *Geography*. Albert was quietly making a playhouse of moss and bits of colored glass under a tree when Mr. Gamble drove up in a hired buggy. And suddenly Mary Bethune saw the place through his eyes—in all its shabbiness and poverty.

James Gamble looked over the scene. "Where is the school of which you want me to be a trustee?" he asked.

Her hopes fell. She realized that she had spoken of the school as she meant it to be in the future. It was all so real to her that she had made it real to him, as if it actually existed.

"Where is the school?" he asked again in a puzzled voice.

Mary McLeod Bethune looked up undaunted. She dusted the flour off her hands, and pulled down her sleeves. "In my mind, in my spirit," she answered. "I'm asking you to be trustee of a glorious dream, trustee of the hope I have in my heart for my people."

Gamble was a man used to judging people, used to making big decisions quickly. That was how he managed his business.

He took out his checkbook and wrote a check for one hundred dollars. He made it out to the *Daytona Educational and Industrial Training School, Mary Bethune, President.*

"I'll be back next winter," he said with a half-smile on his face, "and some day, I hope to be present when you dedicate Faith Hall."

11. The Two Marys

IN THE AUTUMN of 1906 Dr. Madison Mason left his new home in Chicago for his annual swing through the Southern states, to inspect schools which would receive contributions from the Freedmen's Aid Society funds. The collections had been larger than usual this year— for a bitter reason. Violent attacks on Negro citizens in Atlanta had shocked people into the realization that all was not well with the Negro in the South.

"Leave the problem to us," the Southern whites had insisted for a generation. "We understand the colored people. Leave everything to us and all will be peace and tranquillity."

In vain colored people had called attention to the kind of "understanding" that segregation had brought about.

"I am a colored woman, wife and mother," wrote a correspondent to a New York paper, describing conditions in the South.

"[The Southern whites] admit that they know us in no capacity except as servants, yet they say we are at our best in that single capacity. . . . The Southerners say we Negroes are a happy, laughing set of people, with no thought of tomorrow. How mistaken they are! . . .

"I know of houses occupied by poor Negroes in which a respectable farmer would not keep his cattle. It is impossible for them to rent elsewhere. . . .

"Many colored women would deny themselves some of the necessaries of life if they could take their little children to the parks of a Sunday afternoon and enjoy the cool breezes and breathe God's pure air for only two or three hours; but this is denied them . . . Pitiful, pitiful customs and laws that make war on women and babes! . . .

"The white criminal cannot think of eating or sleeping in the same part of the penitentiary with the Negro criminal . . . the dead white man's bones must not be contaminated with the dead black man's!"

The nation as a whole had shut its eyes to the lynchings, the chain gangs, the leasing of convicts; to the denial of educational opportunities; to the wretched living-conditions of the sharecroppers on the cotton and tobacco farms; to the disease-breeding shacks in the back alleys of the towns.

A new South was rising from the destruction left by the battles of the Civil War. The countryside was beautiful once more; the cities flourished with new industries, new schools, handsome new homes—for the white population.

A new South was coming into being, but at last whites in the North, and a few in the South itself, had begun to ask themselves whether it was a better South—or only different. In this changed atmosphere, Dr. Mason had found it very easy to raise money to support mission schools. Thoughtful church members were bestirring themselves again to help educate the inheritors of the conditions of slavery.

Knowing the tremendous need, Madison Mason was thankful. Yet he was not easy in his mind. Since coming to Chicago he had seen an alarming spread of Jim Crow sentiment. No legal bars had been set up. No humiliating Colored and White signs appeared in public places. But slowly, steadily, Negroes in the city were being segregated and put into a ghetto—not the newcomers from the South alone, but the older citizens, too, who had come to think of themselves primarily as individuals, as Americans, and only incidentally as Negroes.

Dr. Mason was one of this group. He had gone to great lengths to protect his own family from being hurt by this spreading disease of Jim Crowism. When mixed neighborhoods such as they lived in began to be frowned on, he had quietly arranged to buy the houses on each side of his own. As a landlord he could ensure friendly neighbors. When he heard that Negro children were being taunted and insulted in the public parks, he had built a tennis court in his own back yard for his daughters and their schoolmates.

He wanted his girls to have a happy childhood. Time enough when they were grown, he thought, to take on the responsibilities and humiliations of being colored Americans. But the events of the last year had raised doubts in his mind. Had he kept his own children, his gay, intelligent girls, away from the turmoil of life too long? Twenty thousand Negroes lately from the South lived a few blocks away in the slums of "Bronzeville." They were strangers to his daughters. He and his wife, Mary, had made no friends among them. None had been invited to his pleasant home.

The position that he held, as head of the Methodist Episcopal Fund for Southern Education, had never before been filled by a Negro. His associates in his work were white. In the town where he had grown up, in the schools which he had attended, he had rarely had reason to think of himself as a person apart. His warm, generous, gentle wife had somewhat the same background. They had married very young and had been free to choose their friends, not by the color of their skin, but by community of interest.

His girls knew they were colored, of course, but it meant no more to them than that some of their friends were blond, some red-haired, some brunette. Not one of them knew, really, what it was to be a Negro! They had never had to struggle for an education, never been refused entrance to a theater; they had never seen Jim Crow signs in public places, or ridden in a Jim Crow car; never heard the clanking of irons when the chain gang passed by, never seen Negro prisoners herded by a white guard with a gun. They had never seen—and pray Heaven would never see—a dark form that had once been a living being, hanging from a tree by the roadside.

Dr. Mason had seen all these things in his work for the cause of Southern freedmen. But on this trip in 1906 what he saw struck home more sharply. Perhaps that is why, when he came to Daytona, he acted with such speed and determination.

He had heard from Lucy Laney that Mary McLeod Bethune was starting a school of her own in Florida, and doing a remarkable job on a shoestring. He recalled the tall, young teacher with the sparkling eyes and deep, melodious voice.

When his tour took him to Palatka, he was surprised to see Mary's husband.

"I thought you'd be in Daytona. Miss Laney told me about Mrs. Bethune's new venture."

Alburtus shook his head and sighed. "You know how Mary is—bent on having her own way, and foolhardy. But she'll have to find that out for herself. That school won't work there in Daytona. You can't start a school with no money and no pupils and have it amount to anything. She'll come back sooner or later, content to settle down."

Madison Mason made no answer, but he determined to go to see the new school for himself. He put Daytona on his schedule, and after a stop at Cookman Institute in Jacksonville, took the daycoach down the coast.

He came into the beautiful resort town of Daytona Beach at twilight. The gas lights were aglow, forming pools of color against the tropical brilliance of bougainvillea and hibiscus planted around the station.

The hack-driver knew where the Daytona Educational and Industrial Training School was.

"It's across the river, down on that point of land by the ocean. I know Mrs. Bethune that runs it. She brings her girls to my church to sing some Sundays. I hear she's a Presbyterian but she don't play no favorites. Our children are done grown, but my wife joined up with the Mother's Club Mrs. Bethune started. She's something, that Mrs. Bethune. Daytona ain't been the same place since she come to town. Here you are, sir, right at the door."

The driver drew up before a whitewashed cottage, and Dr. Mason walked up the steps. The door was opened by a young girl. Her cheeks were tear-stained and she answered his questions in little gasps.

"Yes, sir, Mrs. Bethune's home. But I don't know as she can see anybody. She's hurt. She fell down the back steps yesterday. Hurt bad, it seems like."

"Have you had a doctor?"

The girl shook her head. "They ain't—I mean there isn't—no colored doctor in town and the white doctor Mrs. Keyser sent for—"

"Who is Mrs. Keyser?"

"She's our new teacher. She wanted Mrs. Bethune should go to a hospital. Mrs. Keyser, she don't understand about Daytona. Us don't have no hospital."

"You mean there's not a hospital in Daytona? That's unbelievable!"

"They's—there's a hospital, yessir. A white folks' hospital—don't take colored. That's what I was tellin' Mrs. Keyser. I knowed because my papa tried every way to get Mama in a hospital last year, before she died. But Mrs. Keyser, she's from New York. She said same as you. Didn't believe it until Mrs. Bethune told it herself."

Madison Mason came into the hall and closed the door. He could see a cluster of girls and one little boy in what was probably a classroom—packing-box desks, and a blackboard on one wall with spelling words written in a firm, round hand. Over the door was a motto written on a piece of cardboard: Enter to learn. Depart to serve.

A young woman in a black dress detached herself from the group and came forward.

"I'm Frances Keyser," she said. "Mrs. Bethune has met with an accident—perhaps if you wanted to leave a message—"

Dr. Mason introduced himself and after a few minutes' talk with the young teacher, made up his mind. One of the girls was sent to the livery stable to bring back the hack. Another was dispatched to the railroad station to find out about the next train going north. He discussed arrangements for carrying on the school with the young woman from New York. Frances Keyser had only been in Daytona a week or two, but she struck Dr. Mason as highly competent. He gave her money for food, for rent, for any other expenses.

Before midnight he was on the train with Mary Bethune, taking her to his home in Chicago. At Jacksonville, when they changed trains, he telegraphed his wife.

Mary Mason was at the station in Chicago when they arrived the next afternoon. She had a carriage waiting. A room was already engaged at Christ Hospital. Mrs. Mason had seen to everything, even to putting a bouquet of roses in the hospital room.

Mary Bethune had never been looked after like this before. All her life, she had been the one to take responsibility. For the first few days she was too dazed with pain and shock to notice much of anything. Then the pain was gone and there was only the discomfort of having her arm in a cast.

She had only to lie back in the hospital bed and receive the admiring visits of the Mason family. Dr. Mason had gone back to his duties, leaving his "two Marys," as he said, to take care of each other. Mrs. Mason brought the three older girls, one by one, to meet the teacher from Florida. Only the youngest, six year old Mame, was missing. She was too little to be brought to a hospital and waited impatiently at home for a glimpse of the patient.

"Mrs. Bethune is very big," Maine's mother explained. "Her skin is very black and her face—is not pretty. But she is Papa's friend. . . . She teaches school way down in Florida."

Mary Mason always prepared her children carefully for each new experience. The world outside her home seemed harsh and she was a little afraid of it, not for herself, but for those she loved. In the world she lived in, shades of color had come to matter. Books, magazines, newspapers, the theater—everything had taught her to shy away from all reminders of slavery or of an African heritage.

But something in her was stirred by this stranger who was no older than herself, yet seemed as old and wise as Mother Earth—as if she and God were partners.

Mary Mason need not have prepared the little girl so carefully. Three days later, Mary Bethune came into the room. She was, it is true, nothing to look at. She had grown stout in the last year or so. Her clothes were worn and shabby. Her face was homely. No, Mary Bethune was not much to look at. She was something to feel. There was a warmth and dignity about her person that children responded to.

"This is my little Mame," Mrs. Mason said. "Mame, this is Papa's friend—"

"I know," Mame ran forward. "It's Mother Bethune!"

The Masons' home was beautiful—silver candlesticks and linen tablecloths reminded Mary of Scotia. There were other things, too—shelves of books up to the ceiling, pictures on the walls. A piano in the parlor. Hot running water and a porcelain bathtub set high on four iron legs.

"When I build Faith Hall," she said to herself, I'll have hot running water."

And Mary Bethune enjoyed the city life. For all that she had spent a year in Chicago at the Moody Bible Institute, she knew only one aspect of the city. Her mind had been on the heathen in Africa waiting to be converted, and on the kingdom of Heaven. But God had created this world, too. He had created Chicago, and Mary Bethune opened her heart to it.

She went with Mary Mason and saw her first play on the stage. She went to hear the Fisk Jubilee Singers and came back to the Masons' and sang until midnight while Mary Mason picked out the tunes on the piano. (Mrs. Mason played Schumann and Bach beautifully, but she had never played spirituals before. She had always felt that they were listened to as curiosities, that they were used to lower the dignity of the Negro people. When Mary Bethune sang, she realized their beauty and their dignity.)

Mrs. Bethune discovered Jane Addams's settlement house and picked up a dozen ideas that would work in Daytona someday, after Faith Hall was built. She sat one whole day in the public library reading Dr. DuBois's book, *The Souls of Black Folk*. Somehow, she had to get a copy for her History class. And Lucy Laney must have it—or maybe she already had. There wasn't much about the Negro that escaped Miss Laney.

With her arm still in a sling, Mary Mason's sealskin cape over her cotton dress, and the Mason girls tagging at her heels, Mrs. Bethune stalked through the crowded slums of "Bronzeville," stopping to talk to a dozen people in every block.

"Why did you come to Chicago?" she asked a boy carrying a bucket of coal across the sidewalk.

"Poor white trash were awful mean where we come from. Here, you ain't afraid to breathe."

"How do you like it here?" she asked a woman who said she came from Memphis, Tennessee.

"Well, I'm cold sometimes and sometimes I'm lonesome. I came, reluctant. My boy pestered me so's he could go to high school. When I got here and got on the streetcars and saw colored people sitting by white people all over the car, I held my breath. I thought any minute they would start something. Then I saw nobody noticed where anybody sat and I just thought this was a real place for colored people."

"Why did I leave Georgia?" The boy who served them in the ice-cream parlor grinned. "Always liked Chicago, even the name, before I came. Anyways I was tired of having to give up the sidewalk for white people. Where I come from, if you went to an ice-cream parlor, you came outside to eat. Besides, next year when I'm twenty-one years old, I'm going to vote!"

Her weeks of convalescence in Chicago were richly rewarding. Best of all, in Mary Mason she had found a rare friend. But the day she went back to the hospital to have the cast removed from her arm, she announced that it was time she went home.

"Why?" Mrs. Mason spoke quietly. She had known this moment would come, had discussed with her husband in letters the thing she meant to say. "Why do you go back at all? Except to close the school and get little Albert, of course. Stay with us. You could easily get an appointment to teach in a public school at a decent salary."

"Are you tempting me with the fleshpots of Egypt, lady?" Mary laughed. "I admit I've enjoyed eating high on the hog!" She was moved by her friend's offer of a home, of comfort and security, as only a person could be who had known years of struggle and hardship.

But Mary Mason was not to be turned aside with a laughing answer. "Your son could get an education without struggling for it," she said. "And there's plenty to be done right here in Chicago—you've shown me that. You want me to make friends with the people in Bronzeville. Well, then, stay and teach me how! Why go back South where people don't care whether you live or die? A place where you can't get into a hospital, because your skin is black!"

Mary Bethune put her arm affectionately around her friend's shoulder. Not since the days of her childhood had she been surrounded with such love as in this house of strangers.

"You were born in the North, Mary Mason. And as you say, there's a heap to do up here. But I was born in the South. It's my home. That's where my people are. There are maybe forty thousand of our people in Chicago. Eight hundred thousand or so in the whole of the North. Eight *million* in the Southern states, still trying to pull ourselves out of slavery. I almost left once, when I thought the Lord had called me to Africa. Now I know better."

"But the injustices, the persecution, the poverty, the insults!" The gentle brown eyes were filled with tears. "How can anyone like you stay in that benighted land?"

"*Eight million* can't leave! I know how bad the conditions are. I'll stay and change the conditions. While there's one girl in a log cabin eating her heart out because she can't read, I'm staying. And if the whites won't let us in their hospitals, I'll just have to build one. I already decided that, the first day I was in that bed at Christ Hospital. In my mind's eye it's built already—with clean, comfortable beds, an operating room, nurses—a place where even sickness can have dignity."

Mary Mason gave up. "You have to go, I see that. And you'll build your Faith Hall and your hospital. I see that, too. You're wonderful!"

"No, I'm not," Mary Bethune answered, almost brusquely. "I'm nothing out of the ordinary. I'm poor and I'm ugly and not awful smart. There's a thousand people with better brains and better education than I have. But the Lord has chosen me for an instrument—and every ounce of Mary Bethune is going to fight on the side of the Lord!"

12. Faith Hall

OF THE NEXT TWO YEARS, Mrs. Bethune herself recounted a hundred small details that she alone could know.

"I begged strangers for a lamp, a bit of cretonne to put around the packing case which served as my desk. I haunted the dump heap and the trash piles behind hotels, picking up cracked dishes, broken chairs, discarded linen, pieces of old lumber. Everything was scoured and mended. This was part of the training: to salvage, to reconstruct, to make bricks without straw. . . ."

She continued to sell sweet-potato pies in front of the big new hotels and to talk about the school to every customer. She didn't wait for them to accept her invitation to visit her school, but brought her pupils to sing outside the gates. She openly thanked the winter visitors for gifts, however small—and prayed God to let the gifts grow larger.

She enlisted colored families in town in her cause. She talked or gave concerts at the log-cabin churches and at the secret societies and mutual-help clubs. She opened the schoolroom three nights a week for adult classes in reading and writing, in mathematics and in civics.

Those civics classes were really lessons in how to go about voting, how to register, how to pay the poll tax—and why it was important to pay it, even if you had to go hungry to do it. Bricklayers, hack-drivers, butlers from the big houses came to Mrs. Bethune's civics class and went out to exercise their rights under the Constitutional amendments, armored against every obstacle. A dozen years before she had a vote herself this crusading woman was beginning to be a political force in the community.

The night classes did something else. They made the colored population in Daytona aware of the needs of the school. Those who worked in "big houses" brought discarded treasure such as last week's newspapers, old clothes that could be made over, old pots thrown away, an ice-cream freezer—and occasionally, an envelope containing money, quietly contributed by some devout white churchwoman who had the heart but not the courage to speak out for educating the children of former slaves.

The contributions the workmen made were even more substantial. It was these men who had whitewashed the cottage after work hours on the long summer evenings, who had built an outdoor kitchen. It was they who now scraped together enough lumber to put up sleeping quarters for Frances Keyser and the two other young teachers Mrs. Bethune had engaged.

In the procession of days, there were a few important highlights—moments of special triumph, of prayers answered in unusual ways. There was the day the box of school Readers came from Lucy Laney—enough dogeared copies to furnish every pupil in the school with a book of her own.

There was the day the Baptist Church got a new organ and gave Mary Bethune the discarded one. And the day the first scholar passed the seventh-grade examination and began to study subjects taught in high school!

And the day, during the short summer vacation, that an invitation came to Mrs. Mary Bethune, Principal of the Daytona Educational and Normal Training School to attend the annual conference on Negro affairs at Hampton Institute in Virginia. A round-trip ticket fluttered out of the envelope. Mrs. Bethune never knew who sent it. She thought it was probably her "trustee" Mr. James Gamble. But perhaps it was Mary Mason's doing.

Mary Bethune sat inconspicuously in the back row, seeing no one she knew, yet not feeling herself wholly a stranger. Where there was life and thought, where people had their faces turned to the future. Mrs. Bethune felt at home. This was as true when she sat in the back row of this, her first big conference, as in later life when her place was on the platform, her name a byword, a symbol.

She could feel ideas shooting out like sparks from every mind in the hall—minds speaking to minds, having a common goal. She wondered how it would feel to be up on that speaker's platform pouring out your ideas, not having to keep them pent up behind your lips.

She got a chance to talk at the long lunch table. Carrie Walker had come alone to the conference, too. She wanted to see what it was all about. But this well-dressed young woman didn't share Mary's exalted ideas about the value of education.

"America doesn't respect anything but money," she declared. "You can struggle along sending out teachers, cramming book learning into children that haven't got shoes. What our people need is a few millionaires. Before I die, I'm going to make a million dollars."

"I'd rather make a million readers," Mary Bethune I declared flatly. "I'll do it, too, God willing."

Some people would have called their talk the bragging of children, the stuff tall tales are made of. "A million dollars"—"a million scholars." Two different dreams, but both sprung from the American soil. Both were rooted in a single desire: to be part of the America that was their native land.

Common sense would have reminded these two obscure, penniless dreamers that the day of miracles was over. Common sense would have advised Mary Bethune and Carrie Walker to aim somewhat lower, to cut their cloth to fit a lesser pattern.

Indeed, the two young women ended by laughing a little ruefully at themselves.

But thirty years later, when these American dreamers met again, Carrie Walker was America's first Negro millionaire. And Mary McLeod Bethune was administrator of the minorities division of the National Youth Administration, which in one year alone gave schooling to 600,000 children and in the seven years of its existence well overshot the million mark.

The conference at Hampton was more than a bright interlude. It was nourishment to Mrs. Bethune's spirit. Her high task and noble purposes drew strength from the knowledge that she was not alone. She came back believing that her school in the four-room cottage on the oceanside was but one wave that made up a surging tide coming in on the sands.

"There were the usual factions at the conference," she said, talking it over afterward with Mrs. Keyser. "I could feel the undertow of tension between those who leaned toward Booker T. Washington's way and the Northern scholars. Neither DuBois nor Monroe Trotter was there, but they had plenty of spokesmen for 'the higher learning.' "

"Greek *or* a toothbrush," Frances Keyser teased.

The discussion of the two opposing philosophies of education and how the Daytona Educational and Industrial Training School could have the best of both had begun the first day the two women had met.

156

"God intends me to be a bridge between the two factions," Mary Bethune said serenely. "Let's get on with the plans for next term."

It was almost time for school to begin again. Once more Mrs. Bethune took to exploring the back yards of the hotels and the dumping ground on Oak Street to see what could be salvaged to make the school more livable.

One day when she was filling a gunnysack with moss from the huge liveoaks on the dumping ground, the owner of the land happened by. The man pushed his straw hat to the back of his head and eyed Mrs. Bethune with open curiosity. Undaunted, she finished stuffing the gay stringy moss in her sack. Then she looked up and bowed.

"Good evening, sir," she said, as humbly as the white man could wish from a big black woman trespassing on his property. "I was just admiring the fine, old trees on this lot. It's a pity so much of the land is swampy. I'm thinking of enlarging my school and I'd like to have a grove of liveoaks like this on my campus."

"You're that Mary Bethune, I reckon. I've heard your little darkies singing hymns outside Mr. Flagler's hotel. What makes you think this lot is for sale? What makes you think I'd sell it to a colored school if it was?"

"Well, is it? And would you?" Mary's businesslike questions took the man by surprise. The truth was, he had been wanting to get rid of this eyesore for years, but even with Daytona Beach booming as it was, he hadn't found a buyer.

He took off his hat and scratched his head. "Land around here's going sky high," he temporized. "I couldn't take less than a thousand dollars for this acreage."

Mary's eyes gleamed. She loved to bargain. Casually she introduced a mythical patron into the conversation. In her mind's eye he resembled Mr. Gamble presenting her with that first check of one hundred dollars.

"A white gentleman, one of the patrons of my school, said this lot wasn't worth more than a hundred dollars. Full of mosquitoes and trash, the way it is, he said."

"It's worth five times that amount if it's worth a cent," the man answered.

"It's got a right bad name, sir," Mary put on the cloak of humility again. "I don't know if you've heard, being the owner, but people around Daytona Beach call this 'Hell's Hole.'"

The upshot was that the man agreed to sell the land for two hundred dollars, five dollars down and five dollars every month Mrs. Bethune could find it.

Years later, recalling this moment of victory, Mary Bethune said: "He never knew, but at the time I didn't even have the first five dollars. But I got it, all right, by selling ice cream to the workmen who were putting up some new buildings at the beach."

Some of these men were Mrs. Bethune's students at the night school. When they heard that she had bought "Hell's Hole" for the school building she was always talking about, they set to work after their regular working hours and helped clean it up. Using the tools from their jobs, they drained the swamp in a way that would have done credit to an engineer. They made great bonfires of the trash and buried what couldn't be burned.

Eight-year-old Albert had the time of his life. Every night was like the Fourth of July with the red glow of fires next door, and barbecues and singing.

Mary's heart sang, too, as the native beauty of the land began to emerge. She begged plants, now, and haunted the woods, gathering ferns and wildflowers to grace her campus. All her planting skill before had been out of sheer necessity. Cotton seed in the ground, weed chopping between the rows! Corn, rice, turnips—all through her childhood she had planted and harvested under the threat of hunger. Now, for the first time, she planted for beauty. Only one spot was left clear of vegetation. This was the site of Faith Hall.

The fall rains came and turned the dump heap green. The school term opened with more scholars than the little house could hold. Once again Mary Bethune faced the prospect of finding food enough, books enough, time enough for teaching. Once again, by her magic, she made bricks without straw.

Then, in the middle of the winter of 1908, the future caught up with her. Mr. Gamble had built a winter home in Daytona

Beach and came down for a few months every year. His interest in the school had grown with each visit. He had made a habit of inviting Mrs. Bethune to bring her scholars to his home for a concert. She provided the music; he, the audience. The contributions from himself and his friends went a long way toward keeping the school going.

1908 was different. James Gamble came prepared to do something more substantial. He was not one to waste his money. But all through the summer, he had been unable to get out of his mind the picture of this stalwart woman who talked about God and the Declaration of Independence in one breath and put into song all that her words failed to express. He appeared at the school one day, before Mary Bethune knew he was in town. She was teaching a class in geography. Lacking a big map, she had drawn her own on the blackboard. For a pointer, she used a walking-stick whittled out of a hickory limb.

James Gamble listened patiently until the lesson was finished. Then the class was set to studying and Mrs. Bethune was ready to devote her single-minded attention to her sole "trustee." She led him proudly outdoors to see the transformation of the dump heap, and she regaled him with the story of her bargaining for the land. She knew very well that he liked to hear her stories and repeat them to his friends.

But when they came to the spot Mary had marked off for Faith Hall, he grew serious. He asked detailed questions of just what she was planning. How many classrooms? What about living-quarters? What about plumbing and heating? What about this hospital wing she had mentioned?

Mary could have talked all day. The plan was so clear in her mind that no detail had been overlooked. But after a few minutes' conversation, Mr. Gamble stopped her.

He was satisfied that this dreamer was also a practical businesswoman, capable of directing a big operation.

"You remember my friend Mr. White?" he asked. "A portly, white-bearded man?"

"Mr. Thomas White? Of course, sir." Mr. White made sewing machines. He had sent Mary a machine for her sewing class after seeing the broken-down one these girls were using.

"I have asked White and three or four other friends to meet with you tomorrow." James Gamble smiled. "If you'll have us, we'll serve as your board of trustees. I think the time has come to build Faith Hall."

13. The Seed Ripens

WHEN Mrs. Bethune was a child back in Mayesville on her father's farm, time was not measured by the months nor by the seasons. The year, like Gaul, was divided into three parts—planting time, chopping time, and picking time. The seed of the cotton was put into the plowed earth. The time for that was set by the weather. Weeds growing lusty green among the cotton stalks followed soon enough. The weeds marked the time for getting out in the hot sun with a hoe. Chop. Chop. Chop.

When she was scarcely tall enough for the plants to reach to her shoulder, Mary used to stare at the bolls getting fat and white, row on row, all the way from the house to the swamp. Day after day, she'd stand in the field, watching. And nothing seemed to happen. Then one morning before sunrise, she'd be wakened by her father's exultant shout:

"Everybody up! Praise God, the cottons ready!" The seed, planted an endless time ago, came to fruit all at once.

To Mary McLeod Bethune, the years after Faith Hall was built were like this ripened cotton. The waiting period was over. The seed of her hopes, sown with "faith and prayer and sweat," were bursting with rich bloom.

No sooner had the big four-story frame building been completed than it was filled to overflowing. At the first meeting of the board of trustees after Faith Hall was dedicated, she unfolded a new vision: a brick building this time, a dormitory for the girls, and a chapel so Faith Hall could be used entirely for classrooms. The money was somehow forthcoming—largely through the generosity of Mr. White. By 1911, contractors, masons, carpenters were swarming over the campus. White Hall, as the dormitory was to be called, would be ready for the new term! Every detail was as Mrs. Bethune had seen it in her mind's eye, four years before.

Trustees and buildings—these had been only part of her girlhood vision of a school of her own. The core, the center, was the teaching, to bring knowledge to her people who walked in ignorance. That the soul be without knowledge is not good. The first class had graduated from the eighth grade. This year, the high school would be a reality. History books, science books, Latin and Greek grammars stood ready on the library shelves. Secondhand, dog-eared though they were, the learning of the world was in them. Frances Keyser had seen to that.

That young woman was a gift from God to Mary Bethune. A graduate of Hunter College, in New York, widowed almost immediately after her marriage, she had been prompted to come South by no more than a vague longing to help break down illiteracy. Her experience could not have been more different than Mrs. Bethune's. She had never seen the barefoot children of the cotton cabins, the turpentine camps, the corn fields. They were statistics in Dr. DuBois's reports in the stacks of the Hunter library. They were photographs in Carter Woodson's *History of the Negro*. They were words in the poems of Dunbar and James Weldon Johnson. But Frances Keyser was a scholar to whom statistics and pictures and singing words came alive. There were forty girls crowded into three rooms of a whitewashed shack when she applied to Mrs. Bethune for a teaching position. The books and equipment, according to her standards, were hopelessly inadequate.

But there was a passion for knowledge even in the youngest of the pupils such as she had not seen in any of the other schools she had visited. She had had offers from well-established Negro schools. There was not one in the South that would not have welcomed a person of her education and background on its staff. But she chose to come to work for Mrs. Bethune for $3.50 a month and room and board.

Now, five years later, Mrs. Bethune had put the planning of the courses, the choice of textbooks, the supervision of the other teachers, the "book learning" in Frances Keyser's keeping. She knew that from the day they entered to the day they were graduated the scholars would have the benefit of thorough scholarship and the rich culture that was the birthright of mankind. Greek and a toothbrush . . . Thanks to God—and Frances Keyser—the school could have both.

Not that Mrs. Bethune kept her finger out of the academic side entirely! She was far too bossy for that, and her ideas, her skill in the techniques of teaching too valuable. The emphasis on music and science and on the history of the Negro people in Africa as well as in America were her special contribution. But she could stride into any classroom and know what questions to ask that would test the scholars' understanding of the day's lesson. Her wide, radiant smile was praise enough to last for a week. But woe to the pupil—or the teacher— who was careless or negligent! Did not the Bible say he that is slack in his work is brother to him that is a destroyer? Even when Mrs. Bethune was off about other business, her presence was felt in the classrooms. The girls had only to look up on the walls to read the little messages she had tacked up. Carefully lettered mottoes were always appearing. Many were Biblical quotations or a line from a poem. Others were short, crisp admonitions in the rhythm of her own speech: Blessed is he that readeth. Speak softly, save your voice for songs of praise. Cease to be a drudge, work to become an artist.

The students never forgot Mrs. Bethune's mottoes.

"That one about ceasing to be a drudge and becoming an artist," one of them said, years after she had graduated, "that one was not in a classroom as you would expect. It was in the kitchen, where we learned to bake bread and prepare meals as tasty as they were pretty to look at."

The girls did all the work of the household. An hour a day for each pupil was the rule, for in Mrs. Bethune's mind a broom, a frying pan, and a scrubbing brush were as important as a book in their role of womanhood. Neatness, cleanliness, beauty in the home—these, too, were a kind of prayer to God.

Across the road from the campus, an empty field had been turned into a vegetable garden. The girls did all of the work, and the beans and carrots, the sugar cane and strawberries and sweet potatoes went far toward supplying food for the two hundred people now under Mrs. Bethune's care. They also brought in money. She had built a wooden stand by the roadside and the ladies of Daytona Beach, in white gloves and plumed hats, made a habit of driving up in their carriages or electric broughams to buy baskets of berries or tender carrots pulled fresh while they exchanged a few words with the big, black homely woman with the sun of humanity shining from her eyes.

It was the talk the great ladies came for, more than for the fresh foodstuffs . . . the winter residents from the North quite frankly and normally, but the Southern women almost furtively—denying to themselves that they could draw inspiration and wisdom from a shabby colored woman with a hoe in her hands. But Mrs. Bethune understood.

"They're prisoners of their past—shackled as much as any poor vagrant on the chain gang," she'd say when her teachers grew indignant at their patronizing language and blindness. "They are children of God and will learn to hearken to the speech of friendliness. Hope and wait quietly. Someday these women of ease will have enough of their imprisonment. They will listen with their hearts to the words they hear in their churches, and then you'll see!"

She spoke softly and made friends for the school among the white townspeople when they'd let her. But she could rise up in anger too. And when Mary Bethune got mad, things happened.

Ever since the railroad was finished, she had heard discouraging tales of the turpentine camps that opened a few miles from town. Many of the track-workers had found work in the pine forests where the pitch was distilled. Shanties had been thrown up and the workers brought their families. The conditions they lived under were as bad as slavery—worse perhaps, since under a slave economy it paid the owners to keep their workers alive. The turpentine manufacturers were under no such necessity. There were always more untrained, illiterate colored people who could be enticed from the plantations to any work that offered regular wages. No respectable Negro from Daytona would take work in the camps. The ministers regretted that there were no churches at the camps. The temperance societies, white and colored, grieved over the drunkenness. The white doctors shook their heads over the high death rate. But nobody did anything.

One beautiful Sunday afternoon, Mrs. Bethune had taken Albert and a few of the girls off for an outing up the river. They picnicked near one of the turpentine camps and Mary made up her mind to go in to see the conditions for herself.

She came home enraged and heartsick. That week, she had no smiles for the white people of Daytona Beach who had the power and the money and let other human beings live no better than animals.

"What doth it profit," she read to her students, "though a man say he hath faith, and have not works? If a brother or sister be naked, and destitute of daily food, and one of you say unto them, Depart in peace, be ye warmed and filled: notwithstanding ye give them not those things which are needful to the body: what doth it profit? Know ye not, O vain man, that faith without works is dead?"

After a few days, she had channeled her anger into action. "Neither man nor God has any use for a discouraged woman," she asserted.

The next Sunday, she went back to the camp, armed with her Bible, with medicines, and scrubbing brushes, with slates and chalk and a few first-grade school books no longer needed for her own classes. This was the beginning of the "Bethune Missions." She stirred up a few of the women in the camp. Together, they cleared out a shack and scrubbed it clean. She gathered the ragged children around her and sang to them and read them the story of the infant Jesus, born in a stable. She went from hovel to hovel, encouraging, admonishing, doctoring the sick, and shaming the drunkards. She called a few people together in the shack and led them in hymn after hymn. She read from the Bible and preached a sermon. Before she finished, the room was overflowing with listeners. Men and women were standing deep in the soft pine needles on the earth outside the door. They felt human. They felt part of the world again. This was the kind of thing she had learned to do at Moody Institute; it was like her Sunday school at Haines . . . but it was different, too. The missions Mary McLeod Bethune set up first in the turpentine camp nearest her home and later in four other camps were the fruit of mature experience. The missions were not separate from her own school, nor from the vision she had of what a school should be.

She had, from the first, made the Daytona Educational and Industrial School a center of community life. In establishing schools and singing classes and training home-making for these neglected, isolated, wretched families of "the piney woods" she merely stretched the size of the community. Older girls who were training to become teachers got their practice work by holding classes in the missions for three months out of the year. Girls who were in training as nurses came to the camp missions to care for the sick. The school choir went out to camps singing the same songs that delighted the winter visitors at the fashionable hotels. And Mary herself gained experience and confidence in her powers of organization that would someday be used in a far wider field.

Out of Mary's righteous anger, in these same "harvest years," another great need was filled. Four years earlier, in Chicago, she had determined that Daytona Negroes should have a hospital. "I know conditions are in the South bad," she had said to Mary Mason. "I'll stay and change the conditions. I'll build a hospital, someday."

But even as she made the promise, fulfillment seemed far off in the future. She had talked to the nurses and interns at Christ Hospital and had learned how much more was needed for the care of a patient than just a bed and meals served on a tray. Even to her bold mind, a hospital was too big a dream. When she got back to Daytona, other problems pushed themselves into the foreground, though she didn't forget the need for proper care for the sick. She talked about it to anyone who would listen, especially to a young Negro doctor who had come to practice in Daytona. She went with him before the city hospital board to beg that at least one ward be set aside for the most serious cases. She watched their faces as they listened to the young man's plea. She knew before the answer came that nothing would come of it.

"Why we haven't even got beds enough for our own people. What do you think the taxpayers would say if we went ahead now and spent money on a nig—I mean colored—ward?"

When they came out of the City Hall and trudged back across the bridge to the colored section, Mrs. Bethune tried to comfort the young doctor in his despair. "And the word of the Lord came unto me, saying, Son of Man, prophesy against the shepherds of Israel. . . . .Woe be to you. The diseased have ye not strengthened, neither have ye healed that which was sick. . . . Behold, I the Lord God will strengthen that which was sick; but I will destroy the fat and the strong. I will feed them with judgment!"

"I don't understand it, Mrs. Bethune," the doctor answered. "They're Christians, too—those men back there. And even if they have no mercy in their hearts they ought to have sense enough to know that germs don't pay any mind to Jim Crow laws. . . . What kind of place is our country anyhow? I was born down here in Florida and all the time I was away getting my medical education, I had a hungry longing to get back to the liveoaks and the gray moss and the sunshine. But it's no use, is it?"

Mary Bethune straightened her broad shoulders and looked with compassionate eyes at the dejected figure at her side. To be both an American and a Negro. It was harder for some than for others. The young man could have an easier life somewhere else. But Daytona had need of him.

"You stay," she said, and the words were like a command. "You'll have a hospital."

A few weeks later, one of her own pupils was stricken with acute appendicitis. Mrs. Bethune went to a white doctor at a private hospital and begged him to operate. He agreed grudgingly. But after the operation, instead of a bed in a decent room, Mrs. Bethune found the child on a cot on a drafty back porch. Jim Crow. . . .

Again out of anger came action. Mrs. Bethune found a cottage for sale close by the school. It could be had cheap. But there had to be an operating table, and good lighting and plumbing and beds and sheets and blankets. She sent for the Negro doctor and they figured costs together. Five thousand dollars would do—but she didn't have five dollars that could be spared from the running expenses of the school.

She sat up all night writing begging letters. She wrote to friends in the North, white and colored. She wrote to strangers who were no more to her than names in a newspaper. In a month she had the money. In two months, the house was ready. For staff, she had the doctor, for nurses her own girls who were in the nurses' training course. There were only two beds, but that was two more than any Negroes in Volusia County had ever had. Mary Bethune knelt and thanked God for the ripened seed.

"What are you going to name the hospital?" the girls wanted to know. Mrs. Bethune had been much too busy to give any thought to a name, but now it came to her that she'd like to name it for her father who had died three years earlier.

"McLeod Hospital," she answered. So Sam McLeod, who had been born a nameless slave, gave the borrowed name of his owner to a hospital that was destined to grow and to serve the freedmen of Florida until the city of Daytona twenty years later assumed its obligation and built a hospital for its Negro citizens.

On the day the McLeod Hospital opened its doors, Mary wrote one more letter. She wrote to her mother and enclosed a railroad ticket. Hattie or one of the grandchildren would read it to her and would see that she got safely on the train for Daytona Beach.

Patsy McLeod was seventy years old. She had never been on a train. She had never seen her daughter's school. She had never seen her tall, handsome, eleven-year-old grandson. There had never been any money to spare for visiting. It's true, Mrs. Bethune had a salary. Mr. Gamble and the other trustees had seen to that, but until now she had never thought of using any of it to satisfy her personal wishes. She had sent money when it was needed to her parents, and to piece out Hattie's scholarship the two years she spent at Scotia. She had used her own money to provide for Albert, and next year she was going to send him to Lucy Laney's school because he was getting too old to be at a school just for girls. But the railroad ticket to bring her mother to see her school and the McLeod Hospital was pure luxury.

She'd take her around and show her everything. She'd have the girls give a concert, just for her mother. She'd make her sit idle in the sun and not do any work at all. She'd say, when

Mama's eyes got big with wonder at all that the Lord had let her daughter create: "Do you remember how it was, waiting for the cotton to ripen? How at last Papa used to shout 'Everybody up! Praise God, the cotton's ready'? You remember how, when I was nine years old I picked two hundred and fifty pounds? Well, I'm thirty-six now and all this year my dreams have been ripening. It's picking time, Mama!"

14. "Turn on the Lights"

THE IMPRESSION that Patsy McLeod made on those who met her at the school is a matter of record. Years later, students and teachers alike recalled with vivid pleasure the sight of the frail-looking little lady exploring every corner of the gardens and grounds, listening alertly with head cocked like a bird to Frances Keyser's classroom lecture on the Fourteenth and Fifteenth Amendments, or wistfully fingering the books in the library.

But the interesting thing would be to know how Patsy felt about it all. What was going on in her mind when she sat in the audience of four or five hundred people on Sunday afternoon and watched her daughter lead the exquisitely trained chorus in the very songs she herself had sung in the days of her captivity, on the nights when she found it hard to sleep for worry lest some of her children might be sold away from her? What was it like to know that out of the poverty, the hunger, the contempt, the everlasting washboard and the hoe, had come this eloquent voice, her child, reading the Thirty-Seventh Psalm?

"Trust in the Lord, and do good; so shalt thou dwell in the land, and verily thou shalt be fed.

"Delight thyself also in the Lord; and he shall give thee the desires of thine heart.

"Commit thy way unto the Lord; trust also in him; and he shall bring it to pass.

"And he shall bring forth thy righteousness as the light, and thy judgment as the noonday."

Did Patsy, sitting prim and straight in Faith Hall, think of the time when Mary left school to take her turn at pulling the plow, that spring when the mule died? Did she think of the blue-back speller that used to stay on the shelf next to the Bible? Reading makes the difference. Her long-legged, pig-tailed, homely little girl had been so stubbornly sure of that. But white people could learn to read without having to beg for the learning— and not all of them got wisdom or loving kindness from the printed word. Did Patsy McLeod consider these things as she watched Mary close the Bible and begin her little sermon that was part of the regular Sunday service? Did she glance around the audience to see how the white visitors were taking Mary's plain, blunt words about the duty and responsibility of citizenship?

It is impossible to say what were the impressions and thoughts of this woman who spent half her life in slavery and the, other half keeping her family alive. She left no record of this visit to the school her daughter had created. She could not. It was not the lot of Patsy McLeod to learn to read or write.

Mrs. Bethune's mother came to Daytona once more, shortly before she died in 1915. There were other visitors, too. Miss Mary Crissman had journeyed across the country from Colorado to see the "girl who had made good." Booker T. Washington came, and Mame Mason from Chicago, pretty as a picture at nineteen, just graduated from college and on her way to begin her teaching career, as Mrs. Bethune had, under Lucy Laney.

And Alburtus came at last, handsome and gallant as ever. He spent several months in Daytona Beach. He went fishing with his young son and advised Mary on Albert's future education. He joined his fine tenor voice to the chorus in the chapel. Together, he and Mary pored over the music books she had collected. But the school was not of his creation. He could not find a place for himself in the vigorous, hard-working environment. When the fall term began and their son went off to Haines, Alburtus Bethune left Daytona. Until his death five years later, he taught in a boys' school in Georgia. His letters to his wife were friendly. He conferred with interest and concern about the choice of a college for Albert. But he never returned to the school.

Perhaps with a different type of man, Mrs. Bethune might have made a success in the role of wife as she did in other human relationships. Perhaps not. She was surely capable of deep, warm emotion. She had grown up in a household sunlit with love. But the very qualities that made her great made marriage difficult.

She was possessed by a vision and dedicated to a cause. And, as she herself admitted, she was self-willed and "bossy." In her day and time, only rare good fortune would have granted such a woman the fulfillment of a happy marriage.

In the first decade of the twentieth century the long struggle for a change in the role of womanhood was nearing victory. From the first, the struggle had been intertwined with the battle for Negro freedom. Frederick Douglass and William Lloyd Garrison, the foremost figures in the abolition movement, had fought for the rights of women to take their place as citizens in a democracy. Susan Anthony and Lucretia Mott and Elizabeth Cady Stanton, leaders in the woman suffrage movement, were stalwart abolitionists. Significantly, it was Sojourner Truth, the fugitive slave, who most completely recognized the absolute unity of the two battles. And it was Frederick Douglass who had said: "Freedom begins at the ballot box!"

The Fifteenth Amendment, incorporated into the Constitution five years after the close of the Civil War, gave legal guarantees that no man should be deprived of this unalienable right because of "race, color or previous condition of servitude." Since then, enforcement of this guarantee has been a struggle, never quite won, never quite lost.

But the Negro woman—and the white—were given no such legal base from which to fight. Year after year the campaign for woman suffrage continued. Every year for fifty years members of the National Woman Suffrage Association presented themselves before Congress to demand a Constitutional Amendment similar to the Fifteenth—"No citizen shall be deprived of the right to vote because of sex." State by state, the women organized meetings, parades, bazaars to raise a little money. In the North and West, black women and white united in the battle and victories were won. By 1918, women could vote in fifteen states. In the South, segregation weakened the forces for progress as usual.

In 1912, a Southern Conference for Woman Suffrage was organized. Its members were white. Mary McLeod Bethune joined the Equal Suffrage League which had been organized as a part of the National Association of Colored Women. She read with longing the accounts of the huge mass meetings in other parts of the country.

There didn't seem much that she could do in her own remote corner of Florida. By subterfuge, by threats, by legal trickery, the guarantees of the Fourteenth and Fifteenth Amendments had been all but nullified in Volusia County. Only a handful of Negro men managed to cast a ballot. That she—a Negro and a woman—would ever be free to go to the polls to exercise her responsibility of citizenship seemed a possibility as remote as a flight to the moon.

Then, in 1917, America entered the war which had been raging abroad for almost three years. Against Deutschland über Alles, President Wilson proposed the slogan "Make the World Safe for Democracy."

The words were a potent weapon to fight with, at home as well as abroad. The Nineteenth Amendment to the Constitution, assuring women the right to vote, was passed by the Congress. In August of 1920, in time for the Presidential election, it had been ratified by enough states to become part of the law of the land. Women in the South—Negro women—now had a chance to vote for better schools, for health measures, for lawmakers who would represent the whole people. They had the chance to make the promise of the Declaration of Independence come true.

Mrs. Bethune sang *Year of Jubilee*, rolled up her sleeves and went to work! She counted the obstacles to be overcome. She was aware that for Negro women, the Nineteenth Amendment would be one with the Fifteenth—a thing to be got around rather than enforced.

Florida had a stiff literacy test and a different ballot box for every office. Mrs. Bethune's night classes in reading and civics could take care of that.

Florida had a poll tax. Families whose cash income averaged $500 a year could not spare $1.50 for a man to vote. They'd need twice that now. Mrs. Bethune went to the churches, to the women's clubs. She got out the old bicycle she'd used on her "begging days," when, in the early years of the school, she had gone from door to door in the palm-lined streets of the rich to ask for contributions. Now she pedaled up and down the unpaved streets of Terryville, the Negro ghetto.

"Go without food if you must, but pay that poll tax in the service of the Lord," she exhorted.

Florida took its politics seriously. Each faction beat the bushes for votes—white votes, of course. The re-born Ku Klux Klan tried to make sure that there would be no effort to register men or women with black, brown, or ivory skins.

But quietly, under Mrs. Bethune's prodding, almost a hundred Negroes in Volusia County qualified. Eleven of these were teachers at the school. The twelfth was Frank Wilson, the night watchman. The rest were workers in Daytona—doctors, ministers, brick-layers, taxi-drivers, housewives, cooks in other women's kitchens.

Between registration and election day, Mrs. Bethune was out of town, raising money for the Red Cross. She returned at dusk on the evening before the election.

At the door of the station marked Colored, a jitney cab was waiting. The driver jumped out to help her in. He was a member of her "voters' club." She gave him one of her rare, dazzling smiles, glad to be home again and out of that Jim Crow train.

Daytona Beach looked beautiful. Rain had washed the summer dust off the trees. The flowers around the station glowed under the new electric street-lights.

"All ready to vote tomorrow?" she asked, just to be making conversation.

The driver cranked the Ford and drove a block before he answered. Then he spoke in such a low voice that his passenger had to lean forward to hear him.

"Mrs. Bethune, the Klan was out last night."

"Was anybody hurt in Terryville?"

"They didn't bother coming to Terryville, Mrs. Bethune. They went straight to your school."

Mary Bethune's heart contracted. Her shoulders sagged. She had left two hundred defenseless girls in the care of a handful of teachers—mostly young women from the North. The only man on the campus was old Frank Wilson.

"What happened? Drive faster, can't you?"

"Nothin' happened, Mrs. Bethune. They just paraded up and down in front of Faith Hall and in front of White Hall. Every window was dark. Mrs. Keyser turned out the lights and gathered the girls into the chapel and kept 'em singin' hymns. There weren't no panic or nothin'. Frank Wilson told me. He stood on the steps outside to stop anybody that started in. Fat chance he'da had! But the Klan musta meant it for a warnin' to say they knew you was at the heart of the votin'."

Make the world safe for democracy. Mary Bethune's jaw clamped shut. *Oh, Lord, how long, how long must thy people walk in the wilderness?*

"Mrs. Bethune, what some of us were thinkin is that they'll sure come back tonight. Don't you want that some of us should mosey around?"

"Bless you, no." Mary Bethune did not hesitate. "You come in the morning. Get every one of our people that are going to the polls—the men and the women."

The brakes squeaked as the car drew up at the steps of White Hall. The new brick dormitory had been named for Mr. Thomas White, who had given most of the money but not all of it. Some of the townspeople of Daytona Beach had contributed, too, and at the dedication the mayor himself had spoken. Daytona was reconciled to the school—only she mustn't teach anyone to be a good citizen, she mustn't help anyone exercise the basic right of citizenship. Voting was going too far.

Mrs. Bethune unlocked the door and went inside. The hall was dark, but she could hear voices and the clatter of dishes downstairs in the kitchen and dining-hall. Quietly she went down, and stood for a moment unnoticed in the doorway.

The atmosphere was serene. One of the younger teachers was reading at a long table to the younger girls. In the long, well-ordered kitchen supper was being prepared. There was no sign of fear or tension.

"Mother Bethune!" The girls clustered around her and she took those nearest in her arms, let them feel her love and confidence.

Nothing was said until the evening meal and prayers were over. Then Mrs. Bethune gathered her teachers in her study. "Put the younger girls to bed in the back of the house," she directed. "And turn on all the lights in the front. All the lights. Open the blinds. Sing if you want to. It's choir-rehearsal night anyway. Singing is good. I depend on you to keep spirits high and fear from your hearts, as you did last night."

"What are you going to do, Mrs. Bethune?" Frances Keyser asked quietly.

"Let 'em see me!" Mary Bethune smiled for the first time since she had heard the bitter news. "I'm going to stand where Frank Wilson stood last night. But not in the dark. They are the figures of darkness."

About nine o'clock, she took up her stand outside the door, between the white pillars. In her broadcloth dress and long cape she was an imposing figure. She knew it and was glad of it. She was regarded as a symbol, an instrument of freedom. Tonight she would be a lightning rod.

How beautiful the night! There was no moon, but the lights streaming from the windows fell on the green grass and the lower branches of the oaks, draped in shadowy moss. The honeysuckle was blooming again, ignoring the calendar.

Time passed slowly. It was a long vigil. Perhaps they weren't coming after all. Perhaps she ought to go inside and send everyone quietly to bed.

She had her hand on the door, when, on the street beyond the campus, she heard a sound. There was a flicker of torches.

"If there must be trouble, let it be in my time, that my children may have peace." Somebody—Thomas Paine, she thought—had said that. The words ran through her mind like a song as the white sheets flapped by in the soft November night.

My children. She did not mean her tall handsome son. She did not even mean the little girls sleeping or perhaps lying awake in their neat, narrow beds. These, surely; but also the others, in flimsy shanties, in the turpentine camps and in cotton fields, in tenements and in back streets, in Savannah and Atlanta and Chicago and New York. Black-skinned, brown-skinned—yes, and white-skinned—the children of the white-robed night riders, inheritors of hatred and ignorance. Let all children of God have peace.

The procession halted, turned into the driveway and wavered. Mrs. Bethune saw that one, on horseback, carried some formless sticks clumsily against the flank of his horse. The man raised up, thrust into the ground the sticks that would become a cross.

She could hear low, mumbling voices. Some kind of argument was going on. "God Almighty!" . . . "Uppity nigger. . . ." "You scared of a few lights? . . ." Her shoulders ached from holding them so straight and stiff. She had made up her mind against speaking any of the thoughts that flashed through.

A man got down from his horse. A kerosene can in his hand clinked against one of the stones that outlined the drive. There was a sharp order, and he mounted again, awkwardly because his legs got tangled in the sheet.

The procession wheeled and moved out to the road again. Mechanically Mrs. Bethune counted. Two, four, six on horseback. Eight, ten . . . Eighty white sheets.

"We've got more than that," she exulted. "A hundred registered voters."

Suddenly, out of the night, she saw five or six of the white-robed figures, on foot now, come into the grounds again. One of them picked up the kerosene can that had been forgotten. But they did not leave. They came closer, quite close to the steps, secure in their masks.

"We hear you're teaching colored folks around here to vote." The voice was more menacing than the words.

"We teach civics here, if that's what you mean," Mrs. Bethune answered.

"We've just come to warn you about filling niggers' heads with such ideas."

"But civics is a part of our program, approved by the teaching staff and the board of trustees."

"We can't help that. If you go on teaching it, we'll be back and we won't stop till we burn every building here to the ground."

"Oh Lord, tell me what to do. . . ." Mrs. Bethune bowed her head for a moment in prayer. As if in answer to her plea, the voices of the choir drifted through the window. "My Soul Is Anchored in the Lord, No Man Can Harm Me."

She straightened up and stared defiantly at the hooded spokesman. "If you must burn my buildings, go ahead. But let me tell you. Once you've burned them, I'll build them back again. Then if you burn them a second time, I'll build them again, and again, and again!"

She took a step forward and shook her finger at the men as they backed away. "And all the while I'm rebuilding, I'll be doing something else, too. I'll be troubling Heaven about your dark and evil deeds, and I'll pray so hard that neither you nor any of your offspring will have any peace by day or night."

She paused, startled at her own vehemence. Slowly, the masked men turned and walked out to the road. Mrs. Bethune did not move until they were engulfed by the night. Then she reached out and steadied herself against one of the stone pillars. She was trembling, not with fear but with anger.

Frank Wilson came around from behind a clump of shrubbery. "They gone, Mrs. Bethune."

"Frank, I told you to go to bed and get some sleep."

"Yes, ma'am. But they left the kerosene can again. I'll put it in the storage shed. We can use a can of kerosene."

Mary Bethune looked at the old man who had stood guard alone last night. Was that his first experience with night riders? Or had he known what it was like in an earlier time, when the Klan first marched in the days after slavery? Sometime she'd ask him. Not now. She must go in now to reassure the teachers and the girls. And to prepare for the morning.

"Leave the can here on the porch," she said gently, "where the voters can see it. And keep the lights on. Let them burn until day."

She shivered a little from fatigue as she let herself into the house. In the front room the singing went on.

"Choir practice is over," she said, striding into the room as if nothing had happened. "Get some sleep now. In a few hours more we'll have the blessed sun."

The November morning was warm and bright. Early —as soon as the polls were open—a different procession walked up the road. One hundred citizens of Daytona Beach, Florida, with Mary McLeod Bethune marching at their head like a general. They crossed the bridge over the river to the fire house where the ballot box stood. All the women and many of the men were casting their first vote. *Negroes and Americans.*

15. Opening Doors

THE STORY of the night the Klan paraded to keep Mary McLeod Bethune and her friends from voting spread far beyond Daytona Beach. The Ku Klux Klan was like a new species of vulture in the years after the First World War. The Klan was seizing political power and people were afraid of it. The threat was not against Negroes alone, but against Catholics, Jews, newly arrived immigrants—anyone who was different, anyone who could be kept down. It had spread over the North as well as the South, but as always, the Negroes in the rural South took the brunt of the violence. There seemed no way to stop the beatings and insults and burning of crosses.

Now, in Daytona Beach, Florida, there was one cross unburned! An obscure schoolteacher had stood up to the Klan. People talked about the incident over their dinner tables in Washington, in Chicago, in New York.

"Did you hear about that colored schoolteacher down in Florida? What was her name? Begins with a B. . . ."

"Mary McLeod Bethune—great big woman, black as the ace of spades. Straight out of a cotton cabin—well, not straight out. A friend of mine tells me she can read Latin and quote Thomas Jefferson if she has to. I remember her years ago—I think it was her. Used to sell pies on a street corner in Daytona; sell pies and talk about the school she had. Bought one of her sweet-potato pies one time. Wish I had one right this minute!"

"Well, you can have the pies. I'll take a slice of her courage."

Mrs. Bethune had already done some speaking for the Red Cross, up and down the Atlantic Coast, during the War. Now she was sought out for conferences and public meetings, wherever the welfare of the Negro was being discussed. In her plain, shabby clothes (for in these years she never had any money to spend on herself), she sat on the speaker's platform next to prominent and fashionably dressed clubwomen.

She came in contact with the rising group of poets and artists—the first fruits of education of her enslaved people. She sat there among the great, the talented, the fashionable. And when it was her turn to be called on, she was never nervous, never self-conscious. She never had to fumble for words. She had the kind of eloquence that flowed from strength of conviction. Her earnestness was like a magnet that picked up the hearts as well as the minds of her listeners. Her language was plain with a Biblical plainness. In her deep contralto voice, it sounded like poetry.

"There was a magnificent dignity about her person and carriage," writes Henry Winslow, "that awed her audiences, whether she talked to one person or to many. Through the intonations of her speech, she could build a simple statement into a dramatic charge that brought forth in the minds of her listeners all the calls ever uttered in the tradition of leadership from Moses to modern times."

She found herself speaking before scholars whose books had opened new words to her in her girlhood. She listened as well as talked at these gatherings, and never failed to come home with some fresh idea for action. She had only to hear of a need to begin thinking of a remedy.

"I prayed to God to let me do something about that," she'd say simply, as she outlined some new plan.

She met Dr. DuBois, just back from the Pan-African Congress in Paris, and remembered how his book, Souls of Black Folk, had enthralled her long ago in the Chicago Public Library. When she heard DuBois remark that because he was colored he couldn't even enter a library in the South to borrow a book he had written, Mary Bethune went home and opened her school library to the whole of Florida. For many years this library was the only source of free reading material for Negro boys and girls throughout the state. After Mary Bethune's death, Eleanor Roosevelt commented: "If she had done just this one thing, Mrs.

Bethune would have made a great contribution to American youth."

She vigorously supported Carter Woodson's Association for the Study of Negro Life and History, and her free library made available every issue of the *Journal of Negro History*.

In 1920, Mrs. Bethune was elected to the Executive Board of the National Urban League which had been founded nine years earlier when two organizations, the New York Committee for Improving Industrial Conditions of Negroes and the National League for Protection of Colored Women, had joined forces. When Mary Bethune was put on the Board, the League had branches in various cities where salaried officers sought to broaden employed opportunities for Negroes, to better housing and recreational facilities, and to act as advisers to civic and industrial management. Its leadership was composed of prominent Negroes and whites. At this time, Mary Bethune was the only woman on the Board from the South, where the need for decent opportunities was greatest. It seemed to her worthwhile to spare time and energy for the Urban League.

She attended meetings in support of the National Association for the Advancement of Colored People—the NAACP—whose brilliant lawyers were fighting segregation through the courts. Any fight against Jim Crow was Mrs. Bethune's fight.

She attended conferences of women. It was important to learn to use the victory they had won, to make sure that the women's vote wouldn't become a dead letter in the law of the land.

To the voiceless millions of colored men and women in the South, Mary Bethune was on the way to becoming a symbol. She was a new source of hope and pride. Since Booker T. Washington's death in 1915, they had not had a leader who was one of their own. History was being made for the race, but the leadership was far removed. The leaders had been educated in the big colleges; they lived in the Northern cities; they were well off; they were different. But not Mrs. Bethune! She had done her share of plowing. She knew what it was to go hungry. She had to put up with the day to day insults. She knew what it was to be called *nigger* and *black cow* by streetcar conductors—and never talk back. She knew how it was never to be sure, no matter how careful you were, that you were going in the right door or sitting in the seat assigned to colored. Yes, she lived with Jim Crow and she hadn't let it get her down.

Yet Mrs. Bethune didn't make the mistake that Washington had. She wasn't looking toward a future of everlasting segregation. Where Washington had been willing to accept the idea of white and colored existing "as separate as the fingers of the hand," Mary Bethune called for harmony of the two groups: "Not separate as the fingers of a hand, but with the clasped hand of friendship."

And she was a woman! The women of the South, more than the men, were ready for leadership.

Despite all the outside demands on her time and strength, Mary Bethune's school continued to grow both in size and quality of scholarship. Large sums of money were left to the building fund by wealthy winter residents who had been touched by her early struggles to get the school started. More land and a library building came from one of these bequests and another made possible a new Faith Hall, a fireproof brick dormitory for the girls, to replace the old frame building. Mary also managed to build a little cottage for herself in one corner of the campus. She planned, schemed, cajoled, made one dollar do the work of two for the school's material well-being. With the unfailing help of teachers like Frances Keyser, Portia Smiley, Josie Roberts, Margaret Seville, she pushed forward its academic side as well. Two years of college work had been added to the four years of solid high-school training. One by one the lower grades had been dropped as improvement in the public schools had made it possible for an ambitious child to find a grade school to go to. Only one high school for Negroes had existed in Florida until Mrs. Bethune's school had become a full course high school in 1914. She kept up the training in domestic science and nursing; and her music department was superior to those found in some schools with unlimited means. And with all her activities, she was advisor and mother to four hundred students.

She raised money to add six more beds to the McLeod Hospital. She raised money to pay salaries to the teachers who went out from the school to the turpentine camp missions. She was always having to raise money to pay the running expenses that her low tuition charges failed to cover.

At forty-eight, she seemed to have the vitality of a young woman. She would never admit to herself that she was tired. But on one of her trips to Chicago, Mary Mason lovingly laid down the law to her.

"You're doing too much and you're bearing too great a burden. You've got a gray streak in your hair and you don't take time and money to buy clothes to set off your looks. You're a person, Mary Bethune, not a work-horse!"

Mrs. Bethune laughed. " 'No-wise pretty but strong as a mule'—that's what my grandmother used to say. And there's a lot of plowing still to do!"

Mame Mason Higgins was sitting on the arm of her mother's chair. She had been living at home for the last two years, since the death of her young husband.

She leaned forward earnestly. "You know Mama's right, Mother Bethune. You're a wonderful woman, but the Lord has just given you twenty-four hours in the day, the same as the rest of us."

Mary Bethune looked into the wood fire without answering. She was enjoying their scolding. It was all very well to be the head of an institution and a symbol of progress for the race, but once in a while—when she was here in Chicago with Mary Mason and Mame, or in Washington with little Cecilia Cantcy— it felt good to be just a pampered, middle-aged woman.

And they were right. She did have too much to do. If she could just have the school and not have to think of the bills coming in! And the teachers' salaries to meet. . . . And there were new needs in the back of her mind that she didn't feel able to fill. For one thing, she wanted more boys in the school than the half-dozen that she had admitted. But that would mean a new dormitory, and manual-training workshops, and teachers in the trades.

"What do you think I ought to do?" she asked at last.

"I know what Papa would say, if he were here," Mame Higgins answered. "He'd say consolidate. You've been wanting to make the school co-educational. Why not find a good boys' school that has the backing of the Educational Fund, and bring it to Daytona?"

Mrs. Mason was horrified.

"Turn over Mary's school to other people? After all the work she's done?"

"Only the business end. Mother Bethune oughtn't to have to go on begging for money," Mame insisted.

Mary explored the idea in her mind. There was the Cookman Institute in Jacksonville—small, but a good school. If they wanted to consolidate—if the Methodist Education Board would give a free hand—"I see a procession of young men and women in cap and gown going out from the college, an endless procession going out to serve our people. . . ."

Mrs. Bethune stood up. She put her arm around Mame.

"I can see I need you, my jewel. Come down to Daytona and help me work this thing out."

The younger woman's eyes sparkled. "I'd love it, if Mama can spare me."

"Of course I can't spare you," Mrs. Mason answered affectionately. "What difference does that make if Mary Bethune has set her heart on having you? You know she always gets her way."

A year later, Daytona Normal and Industrial Institute was merged with Cookman Institute. Bethune-Cookman College came into being. The land, the buildings, were deeded over to the Board of Education of the Methodist Episcopal Church. Mary Bethune was to be President of the new institution.

She enlarged her staff to include a few men teachers. She chose a man, John C. Wright, as vice-president. Mame Higgins served as Dean of Women, doing everything from seeing that no speck of dust invaded the spotless dormitories to counseling the girls when Mrs. Bethune was away on her numerous speaking tours. But her most important assignment was the one she gave herself: to bring into Mary Bethune's arduous days a little lightness, a little pampering. She waited on her; she read to her at odd moments of the day or night; she chose becoming clothes for her public appearances. She brought into the older woman's personality a zest for enjoyment that had been buried under the weight of responsibility in her early years.

Something else happened to round out Mary Bethune's personality, to enrich her life. A group of friends conspired to give her a pleasure trip to Europe.

For eight weeks Mary McLeod Bethune traveled in foreign countries, a distinguished American citizen. In Rome, an audience with the Pope was arranged for. In London, she dined with the Lord Mayor. In Scotland, the lord of McLeod Castle begged the honor of a visit. In Paris, she was introduced to distinguished African scholars.

Mrs. Bethune met and talked with people from all over the world on this first journey outside her own country. But one small incident that took place in New York a day or two after her return was of more significance in the life of Mary Bethune than the whole whirlwind eight weeks in Europe.

"I can see the focus of what happens to me on the screen of my life," she said. Perhaps that explains why she remembered the luncheon party in New York and told it later in such vivid detail.

Through a mutual friend, she was invited to a luncheon at the home of Mrs. James Roosevelt, the mother of the promising young statesman whose career everyone said had been cut short by a tragic illness. Mrs. Bethune had met Mrs. Roosevelt just before leaving for Europe. She looked forward to seeing her again.

The Roosevelt house was beautiful—as lovely, Mrs. Bethune thought, as any she had seen in the great cities abroad. The drawing-room sparkled with fresh flowers. It smelled of expensive perfumes and kid gloves. There was an atmosphere of leisure and the things that go with leisure. About a dozen well-dressed women were in the room when Mrs. Bethune arrived. A few of the guests were known to her. Most of them were strangers, but she moved from group to group with her friend, relaxed and self-confident.

She had progressed to the far end of the room when there came to her ears the sound of Southern voices. Mississippi, if she was not mistaken—the first Southern accents, except her own, that she had heard for two months. She glanced around. Over by the piano were two recent arrivals, chatting together in lively, animated tones.

Mrs. Bethune was aware of the exact moment when the short, plump blonde caught sight of her. Eight weeks of freedom from Jim Crow fell away under those piercing blue eyes. That familiar look which set her apart as alien in the land of her birth was sometimes a painful experience. Sometimes the eyes were furtively kind, sometimes they were insolently cruel. The eyes that stared into Mrs. Bethune's across Mrs. Roosevelt's drawing-room were horrified. They were not kind and didn't intend any kindness.

This was a *luncheon* party. Guests would sit down and break bread together. All fifteen of them, at the same table. And one of the guests was *colored*. Mrs. Bethune knew what was being said in the whispered conference by the piano as surely as if she were eavesdropping. Of all the Jim Crow taboos enforced in the Southern states, the most inexorable was the taboo against eating together. At the very least, a white Southerner who broke the taboo could be socially ostracized. Some had lost their jobs. Others had been tarred and feathered and driven from their homes as "nigger-lovers."

On occasion, Mary Bethune could fight against Jim Crow practices with all the force of an Old Testament prophet. But she had a great sense of time and place. The important thing now was to save Mrs. Roosevelt from embarrassment.

The easiest thing would be to think up some excuse to leave; but the butler was already hovering in the doorway waiting his opportunity to announce luncheon. It was too late to act. An audible gasp came from the blonde by the piano. Mary Bethune braced herself; a great sadness swept over her. *How come, America, how come?*

But she hadn't counted on the stubborn Roosevelt spirit. The mother of Franklin Roosevelt could dominate a situation when she wanted to. She came up cordially. "Shall we go into the dining room, Mrs. Bethune? I'm so happy that you could be with us." She led the way to the table. "Sit here, at my right, please," she said, indicating the place of the guest of honor.

A tall, quiet, angular young woman took the chair at Mrs. Bethune's right. Mrs. Roosevelt leaned forward. "I don't think you have met Mrs. Bethune, Eleanor. This is my daughter-in-law, Frank's wife, Mrs. Bethune."

Down at the other end of the table, the two Southern "ladies" took their seats in grim silence, unaware that they had inadvertently helped to change the course of American history. When, two decades later, the United States Senator from Mississippi bitterly proposed that Eleanor Roosevelt be made Queen of Africa, he was assailing the fruits of the First Lady's friendship with Mary McLeod Bethune.

The two women would probably have met in any case. Mrs. Bethune would, in the dramatic years to come, have undoubtedly found herself on many occasions in Eleanor Roosevelt's presence. But whether the wife of a President—even in the period of history in which Franklin Roosevelt held office—would have had the understanding and the will to promote the welfare of millions of colored Americans as Eleanor Roosevelt did is another question. In the opinion of many people Mrs. Roosevelt's remarkable perception of the problems of the Negro citizens in the South grew out of the friendship with just one of their number—Mary McLeod Bethune. And the friendship began at this luncheon table.

With Eleanor Roosevelt and Lillian Smith

Small talk had never come easily to Eleanor Roosevelt, but she had no difficulty finding things to say to Mary Bethune. They talked about her crossing—about the pounding tides on the beach at Daytona, about the rocky island waters where Franklin Roosevelt had loved to sail and swim. They talked about housekeeping, about Paris, about Roland Hayes's concert the night before. It was not until the meal was almost over that Mary Bethune permitted herself to glance down the table where her fellow Southerners were toying unhappily with the food on their plates.

"I guess they're not hungry," she murmured. "Poor things. It must be awful to be imprisoned in a lot of taboos. I sometimes think it's worse for *them* than for us. To be Americans and bigots doesn't work."

Eleanor Roosevelt looked searchingly at the woman of another race by her side. She felt a great desire to see the situation through the eyes of Mary Bethune. What was it that let her hold her head so high?

Mrs. Bethune answered the unspoken question. "I believe in God," she said, "and so I believe in Mary Bethune. Reinhold Niebuhr put it another way. Do you know his prayer? 'God give me the serenity to accept that which cannot be changed, the courage to change that which can be changed, and the wisdom to know one from the other. "

"I see," Mrs. Roosevelt's eyes lit up. "The condition of colored Americans is something that can be changed."

"It's got to be," the other woman replied. "It's too late to wipe out the Declaration of Independence."

16. The Women Take a Hand

MARY BETHUNE, refreshed and confident, returned to Florida to prepare for the new term. It was a time of mounting prosperity in the state. The coast land opened up by Flagler's railroad was flourishing. New resort towns were being laid out. Empty fields were bought, sold, traded at city prices before the cement sidewalks laid down were dry enough to walk on. Profit was piled on profit by winter residents and native Floridians alike.

The colored people got a trickle of the easy money. Their labor was in demand. Even at the low wages paid them, their families could eat decently and clothe themselves in something other than cast-offs. They could afford to let their children go to school.

Bethune-Cookman College had no trouble enrolling as many students as it could accommodate. When money for a new building was needed, Mrs. Bethune made her needs known to the patrons among the wealthy winter residents. James Gamble was dead but the other trustees he had found for her school remained her faithful supporters. She was able to add a new wing to McLeod Hospital, and to build a science laboratory. She was able to raise the salaries of her teachers.

In 1924 Mrs. Bethune was almost fifty years old. She had succeeded against tremendous odds in building a center of education that sent out well-trained teachers, nurses, craftsmen to every corner of the South.

Mrs. Keyser, Mame Higgins, Bertha Loving, her devoted secretary, had looked forward to seeing "Mother Bethune" settle down in her little cottage on the edge of the campus and enjoy the fruits of her years of toil and sacrifice.

"Of course, we should have known better," Mame groaned, when, a few weeks after her return, Mrs. Bethune strode into the dining-hall at breakfast time with the gleam of battle in her eyes.

In spite of all the prosperity Mary Bethune was not happy with conditions in Florida. It is true that a sympathetic state superintendent of education had managed to open a few more elementary schools in the rural districts and get a little more pay for the colored teachers in the public schools; but in all the state of Florida, there was no public high school. There was no public library from which a single Negro boy or girl could borrow a book; no public hospital; no provision for delinquent young people if they happened to have dark skin. The shanties inside the barbed-wire of the turpentine camps were as wretched as ever, and when the workers tried to better their conditions by forming a union, their organizers were beaten and driven away.

For a Negro to vote was to risk his job and even his life. The Ku Klux Klan was more powerful than ever in politics. "For God, for country, and keep the nigger in his place," was the Klan's slogan—and its men got themselves elected.

It was no wonder the young veterans who had fought to "make the world safe for democracy" were leaving the state, going north or west, to New York, to Detroit, to Chicago, to California. Maybe they would better themselves—but the South was the loser. The South that could be so beautiful and was the grave of so many dead hopes. This was Mary McLeod Bethune's greatest concern.

"I'll stay and change the conditions," she had promised herself many years ago. However, all that she had accomplished suddenly seemed small when measured against the great need.

Where millions were suffering, she thought, millions must meet the challenge. Who knew the problems better than the womenfolk? She thought of her mother, her grandmother, and all the women like them. ("If we have the courage and tenacity of our forebears who stood firmly like a rock against the lashings of slavery and the disruptions of Reconstruction," she wrote years later, "we shall find a way to do for our day what they did for theirs.")

"We've got to get our womenfolk together," she announced firmly to the three younger women who were waiting to hear what battle she was girded for. "I see hundreds of courageous, troubled women, alone or in their little clubs over the South. I see them coming together in one great army to fight for justice. I see the Negro women of the South in a federation!"

In the North and West, the Negro women had banded together into a federation of clubs. Through numbers and organization they were making their voices heard for better housing, for jobs. They were training their members to assume the responsibilities of citizenship. Mrs. Bethune had met the founder of the National Association of Colored Women, Mary Church Terrell. A wonderful woman, doing a wonderful work. But the Association could hardly be said to speak for the nation, when the millions of Negro women in the South were not represented.

Mary Bethune spent the next weeks dictating letters to Miss Loving. She sent invitations to church societies, to mothers' clubs, to little social clubs scattered over the South, urging them to send delegates to a meeting at the college to organize for action.

The Southeastern Federation became a part of the National Association of Colored Women. Mrs. Bethune was elected president. She made the organization an instrument for education, for bringing the condition of the unconsidered Southern Negroes to the attention of the rest of the country. She spoke wherever she was asked, to ten women or to a thousand throughout the South, from the Carolinas to Texas. Her speeches were not reported in the white newspapers of the South. But news of them seeped through the wall of silence.

Among a few thoughtful white people there was a stirring of conscience. A social worker here and there, a few teachers, the ministers of a few rural churches used what influence they had to better conditions in their own communities.

The new organization was like a fresh wind blowing. In two years the Southeastern Federation became a force in the National Association of Colored Women. In 1928, Mrs. Bethune was elected president of the entire Association.

The biennial convention was held in California. Delegates representing almost half a million members were gathered in the Civic Auditorium in Oakland when Mary Bethune stood up to make her inaugural address.

She was as handsomely dressed as any woman in the hall. (Mary Mason had seen to that, in the few days that Mrs. Bethune had stopped over in Chicago.) She was a queenly figure in her big picture hat and long black satin dress with flowing sleeves.

She looked around the hall, exulting—not at the honor done her but at the progress her people were making. Little more than half a century had gone by since Emancipation. Some of the women sitting in the auditorium had been born in slavery. Almost all of them had had to struggle against obstacles that would have crushed a weaker people. Yet there they were, in this great public hall, well-dressed, well-informed, ready to move forward as citizens of the most powerful and prosperous country in the world. A country founded on unalienable rights ... on government of the people, by the people, for the people .. . but yet under the shadow of her own section of the country that denied the promise of the Declaration of Independence, that denied the Constitution under which they lived. She was acutely conscious of her Southern background as she rose to speak. She knew that there were critical eyes looking at her, even as they applauded, eyes that doubted the leadership of a woman out of a cotton patch.

She began quietly. She spoke of the accomplishments of the organization in years past. She spoke of faith in America's future. "Those who are strong enough to accept the rich understandings of human experience are on the road to loftier living. We have not come this far alone. We are standing upon the shoulders of those pathblazers who pioneered with such devotion to make our way easier. The foundations laid by Harriet Tubman, Sojourner Truth, Jane Addams, Lucy Laney, Caroline Catts, Ida Wells-Barnett, Mary McDowell, and Mary Church Terrell give me greater impetus and determination for making decisions about opening doors for my people, or about standing before the closed door of opportunity waiting for justice, or about changing the jeers and sneers of the impulsive, unknowing crowds into praise and repentance."

She had the whole audience with her now. She could feel it. There was always a moment, when she spoke in public, when the minds of her listeners were perfectly tuned to her own. She knew how to seize that moment. She used it now to talk about the problems of the South: the poverty in the midst of plenty, the neglected children, the sickness, above all, the unpunished violence, the lynchings.

"Negro women and their organizations have a tremendous responsibility and opportunity to offer leadership in the struggle for a better life in our homeland. But women know too well the disintegrating effect upon our family life of our low economic status. Discrimination and restriction have too often meant to us broken homes and the delinquency of our children. We have seen our dreams frustrated and our hopes broken. We have risen, however, out of our despair to help our men climb up the next rung of the ladder.

"Be a Daniel," she concluded. "Take the vow of courage. But let the weapons of determination be coupled with the armor of justice and forgiveness."

The journey back across the continent was one long triumph. Mrs. Bethune went from city to city speaking to large and devoted groups.

She came back home—to catastrophe. The rest of the country was still boasting of its prosperity. A Presidential candidate was promising a car in every garage and two chickens in every pot— or two cars in every garage and one chicken in every pot. It didn't matter which, to people who had gone back to living on cornbread and sidemeat, who didn't know where the next month's rent money was coming from. For hard times had hit the east coast of Florida with the suddenness of a hurricane. The whole top-heavy structure of prosperity on the east coast had gone down like a tower of building blocks kicked over by a petulant child.

The colored people in Daytona had shared least in the general prosperity and they were the first to feel the pinch of hard times. The men were no longer needed to lay out roads for unbuilt cities, or to carry bricks for houses that would not be erected. They had gone from door to door looking for odd jobs at any wages. There were no jobs. They lounged on the street corners, idle. Their wives went back to cooking for two dollars a week . . . for a dollar . . . for fifty cents and what left-over food they could carry home to feed hungry children. Opportunities for learning and saving, never great, slipped away.

Bethune-Cookman College cut tuition fees. Even so, many of the most promising students had to drop out that first season. Still, Mrs. Bethune managed to pay the teaching staff and to feed the hungry people who came begging at the door.

By the autumn of 1929 when the stock-market crash in New York woke the whole country to the fact that something was wrong, the colored people in Florida already had lived through many months of destitution. The poor whites were not much better off, but it was easier for them to get on county relief rolls.

There were institutions where homeless children of the whites could be taken care of. There were hospitals where the destitute sick could go—if they were white. At first it seemed that trouble might draw the poor—white and black—closer together. Then, in their frustration and fear, trouble between the groups mounted. Twenty-one Negroes were lynched that year.

Mrs. Bethune wrote letters to the governor. She headed delegations to ask for fair distribution of relief money. As the representative of the National Association of Colored Women, she went to Washington to a White House Conference on Child Welfare.

She spoke eloquently on the need to keep up the schools, to find work for boys and girls just coming out of school with nothing to look forward to. "The plight of the young people is the most dangerous aspect of the present crisis," she said. "If democracy is to be saved it will be by the rising generation."

Although there were other equally eloquent speakers at the Conference, Mrs. Bethune came away compelled to face the fact that the Administration in power was not going to do anything directly to help the people who needed help most.

She came back to Jim Crow land bowed under a great burden. A lot of words had been spoken. But there was little will to do. And there was little understanding of the special problems of the South where young and old among her people suffered not only poverty and idleness, but walked in the shadow of a gun or dangling rope.

In the summer of 1930, from a quarter where it was least expected, there came "a glimmer of light on the horizon of a new hope." White women of the South held two public meetings, one in Atlanta, one in Dallas, Texas. The movement had started in the churches. Teachers and social workers had joined forces with the women of the churches. They were ready at last to speak out, to demand that the unlawful killing of innocent Negroes cease.

Mary Bethune read the report of the Atlanta meeting in the morning paper. The brutal facts which Negroes knew only too well were now spread out for everyone to read. *4,287 American citizens had been lynched between 1885 and 1929. Twenty-one such murders had been recorded in 1929 alone and all twenty-one dead were Negroes.*

The white women of the Southern states passed resolutions. "Lynching," they declared, "is not alone the crime of the ignorant and irresponsible mobs. Every citizen who condones it, even by his silence, must accept a share of the guilt."

Mrs. Bethune read the resolution with tears in her eyes. This was the first step in the direction she had prayed for. God had spoken to the hearts of white Southerners. She called Bertha Loving. Walter White, the Executive Secretary of the NAACP, was from Atlanta, and the Atlanta massacre of 1906 had been a driving force in his life. He would understand the great significance of the meeting. Mary Mason, still unconvinced that conditions down South would ever improve, must be told of this resolution—and Mrs. Franklin Roosevelt at the Governor's Mansion in Albany, New York; Mary Church Terrell and the rest of the executive board of the National Association of Colored Women. All these must be told at once.

Bertha Loving read the account in the paper without great enthusiasm. She did not see in this meeting of a handful of white women anything to get excited about.

"It can't compare to your meeting in Oakland," she said.

Mrs. Bethune explained patiently. "Our troubles won't ever be settled until they are settled down here with the white people of the South and the colored working the thing out together. Separate meetings won't do it. I admit that. But they're a step in the right direction. I thank God for every step. Someday He will see to it that we meet in one hall, together. Our children will go to school together. Together, we will have peace."

17. "Let America Be America"

IN 1932, a popular journalist, Ida Tarbell, wrote a piece naming the "fifty greatest women in American history." Mary McLeod Bethune was one of the fifty. Ten years later, this choice would not have seemed astonishing. Today, it would be expected. However, in 1932, Mrs. Bethune held no office except the presidency of the college she had founded, a college that had just managed to achieve the accredited rank of a high school in Florida. Half a dozen persons in the educational field were far better known. It is true that Mrs. Bethune had served for two highly successful terms as president of the National Association of Colored Women. However, had Miss Tarbell's choice been governed by the influence the Association wielded, she would have named its founder, Mary Church Terrell. If the journalist had intended to testify to the intelligence and talent surging up from the millions so long submerged in slavery, she could have named Florence Mills, Rose McClellan, Ethel Waters, or Marian Anderson.

Mary Bethune was neither an office-holder nor an outstanding creative artist. But if staunchness of spirit, if devotion to the ideal of American democracy, if faith in human beings are qualities that enrich American life, then Ida Tarbell's choice was not only sound but prophetic.

The honor thrilled Mrs. Bethune's friends. It gave the students at Bethune-Cookman something to boast about. Out in Denver, the little old lady who had wanted to educate a girl "who would make good" sighed contentedly and said, "now I'm ready to go on to Heaven." Mrs. Bethune herself was too busy to give this new honor more than passing notice.

Nineteen hundred and thirty-two was an election year, recognized by many as the most crucial election for the Negroes of America since Abraham Lincoln went to the White House. The years of the Depression had taken a terrible toll. From the cities of the North whose factories stood idle thousands of colored families had made their way "home," only to swell the ranks of the homeless and hungry in the rural South. The landowners turned their backs. They had no use for more sharecroppers, or "field hands." It didn't pay to harvest the crops that stood in the fields.

In the Southern industrial cities conditions were as bad. It was estimated that 69 per cent of the colored population was in need of relief and they were still getting only what was left after the white unemployed had 1 been taken care of.

"They admit that the patient is sick with fever," Mrs. Bethune wrote. "Diagnosis reveals that he needs twelve grains of quinine; but they decide that because he is a. Negro, they had better give him only six. They admit that he is hungry and needs to be fed; because he is a Negro, they suggest that half a meal will suffice.

The suffering at every age and every economic level was very great. For Mrs. Bethune, the hopelessness of the young people was hardest to bear. A growing number had been educated in the American ideals of equality under the law—the equality guaranteed by the Constitution and the Amendments. They had been encouraged to look forward to opportunities for their full development as individuals. Now, as Negroes and Americans, they were denied the opportunity to use their training. They were hungry and ragged.

It was a bitter experience to watch the frustration of youth— useful and unused. Mrs. Bethune grieved for each boy and girl as if all were indeed her own children. "Americans said the Negro could not learn and they 'proved' it by restricting his educational opportunities," she wrote later. "When he surmounted these obstacles and achieved a measure of training, they said he did not know how to use it and proved' it by restricting his employment opportunities. When it was necessary to employ him, they saw to it that he was confined to laborious and poorly paid jobs. After they had made every effort to guarantee that his economic and social and cultural levels were low, they attributed his status to his race."

Poor as their chances were for making a living, opportunities to go on with their education were even more ruthlessly curtailed. The white South had never seriously tried to give the Negroes a decent education. Even in the prosperous years, under the system of segregated schooling, public moneys had been allotted on a basis that gave seventy cents out of every dollar to the whites, thirty cents to colored schools and colored teachers. For anything above elementary grades, Negro boys and girls had had to depend almost entirely on private schools.

Now, many private schools were forced to close. In none could more than a fraction of the students pay tuition. It had become a race between education and catastrophe. Bethune-Cookman fared better than most. With the little money that came in, Mrs. Bethune had continued to pay the salaries of her teachers, though she had drawn no salary for herself for more than a year. She had gone back to a regime of "save, scrape, and salvage," raising enough food on the campus farm to keep the students from going hungry.

It was not Florida alone, nor the South alone that was in trouble. The problem was nation-wide, and needed to be tackled at the national level. The national government, she felt, must assume the responsibility for the welfare of the people—all the people.

Franklin Delano Roosevelt was the Democratic candidate for President. Mary Bethune had never met him. But, listening to his voice over the radio, reading his campaign speeches, and knowing his wife, she thought it was possible—just possible—that here was a man who could get America out of the dumps.

It was true that he was the candidate of the party that had stood for every discrimination and degradation of the Negro people since the days of Reconstruction. "Why should we think of leaving the party of Abraham Lincoln and Frederick Douglass for the party of Rankin and Bilbo?" Albert argued, when she said that a change in the government was necessary. Other teachers at the schools and friends she talked to voiced the same hesitancy as her son.

"Frederick Douglass has been dead a long time. So has Lincoln. We'll all be dead unless somebody does something. A man like Mr. Roosevelt, who has known suffering in his own body and risen above it, may reach out to the suffering of the oppressed and hungry."

The four-month interval between the election of Roosevelt and his inauguration was not, for Mary Bethune, a period of passive waiting. She knew that even if Franklin Roosevelt meant what he said in his campaign speeches, he could do nothing alone.

"The real leadership, the push, has to come out of the people themselves," she said to Albert one night as they sat in her study. It was a great comfort to her to have him in Daytona, even if they didn't always see eye to eye.

"Now, Mother, don't get yourself excited. What chance has our race to do any leading? Seventy-seven per cent of us live in the South, right under the thumb of the white supremacists."

"Seventy-seven per cent—that's ten million people! Ten million could have a lot of pushing power. If good is to come out of these years of suffering, we've got to have a new Reconstruction. Here in the backwoods, we've got a lot of unfinished business. We've got to know what we want and we've got to ask for it, loud enough for Washington to hear. And don't forget that the man in the White House and his wife have ears tuned to our voices. Keep reminding yourself that Mrs. Roosevelt has a point of view and an inner knowledge of the problems of the great mass of our people."

The young man sighed. "You mean, she *understands the Negro?* I've heard enough of that all my life. The whites boast that they know us, because we walk down the same sidewalks— or work in their yards and kitchens. How many see us in our homes or churches or places of amusement? Still they 'know' us thoroughly. . . . Looks like you'd have enough to do keeping the college going," he said. "You're wearing yourself out making plans you'll never have a chance to carry out. You're going to work yourself up to another attack of asthma."

Mary Bethune lifted her head majestically. Her eyes blazed. Her hair was almost white now, and the spirit within her had molded her features into a kind of stern beauty. When his mother looked like this, Albert could not help feeling a little overawed.

"You think I dream too big, don't you, son? But all my life I've been aware of moments of great decision. I see a million of our children still without a book in their hands. I see the young people we send out of Bethune-Cookman with their training and education unused and festering from disuse. I pray to God to give me a chance to do something about that. I prayed to have a school of my own and I carried you in my arms, looking for a place to build it. While I prayed, I planned. I'm planning now. I've got to be ready."

The American people have nothing to fear but fear itself, the new President said in his inaugural address. In the spring of 1933, machinery for getting people to work again was set in motion. By midsummer, some factories and steel mills had reopened. Building was resumed. The sound of hammer and saw was heard. People held their heads up again. The Federal Government was giving useful work instead of a hand-out to hungry men and women. Civilian Conservation Camps were opened to take homeless boys off city streets. The old and the sick were given a measure of care. There were rumors that something might be done about various other groups in need of help, but there was nothing definite. Congress debated the establishment of a vast public-works program. Included in the public-works bill was a provision for a separate agency to develop small-scale projects where the talents and experience of individuals could be usefully employed. This was the beginning of the WPA.

In Florida, Mary Bethune dreamed and planned with serene confidence. Her vision was always just ahead. This was perhaps the secret of her greatness: to see a need and to be ready with a clear, definite and concrete plan for action at the moment when it became possible to act.

It was just a year after the inauguration of Franklin D. Roosevelt that a long-distance telephone call came from Washington. Would Mrs. Bethune accept an appointment on the advisory board of the National Youth Administration?

The voice was deep, the accent Southern. In spite of herself, Mary Bethune stiffened. It wasn't that she believed, as many did, that no white Southerner could be trusted to give fair treatment to the Negro. But was it possible that any white Southerner could get far enough outside his background—his history—to do the job that was needed? Mrs. Bethune knew that the National Youth Administration was a division of Harry Hopkins's WPA. It was designed to do something for the young people in the country, those who were in school or just out of school and had never had a chance to get experience enough to get a job. Of these, a large proportion were colored. Why had the President handicapped the working of this great plan by appointing a Southern politician as its head?

The speaker gave his name: Aubrey Williams. Mrs. Bethune had heard good things of him. He had once been the pastor of a small church in the cotton belt of Alabama and then had worked for an organization called the Emergency Work Committee. Still, she hesitated.

"Miss Roche—Josephine Roche—has been appointed co-chairman," the voice continued. (Mrs. Bethune had also heard of Miss Roche. She was in the Treasury Department. What had that to do with young people needing work and hope?) "Mrs. Roosevelt says your advice could be invaluable. We need you, Mrs. Bethune."

"I'll come," Mary Bethune answered. If Eleanor Roosevelt thought she could be useful she would go if she had to walk. Even though the position would be only advisory, even though she'd have to borrow money to get there.

She traveled North in a Jim Crow car to a Jim Crow city. She knew what to expect in the national capital. If your skin was dark and you were not a member of the diplomatic corps of some foreign nation—if you were dark-skinned and American—you could not stay in a hotel; you could not rent a room in certain neighborhoods. You could not eat in a restaurant or go to theaters or get a book from the library. Except in private homes or offices it was hard to find a place where white and black could meet on terms of mutual respect. Mary Bethune had played a small part in the long, courageous fight Mary Church Terrell and the NAACP had waged against segregation at the seat of the national government. She was ready to resume that battle.

But she felt almost at once a change that had come over the city. It was as if a new capital had been created side by side with the old.

"This is what Jefferson and Banneker and Washington and L'Enfant had in their minds," she said to herself, as she strode along the broad avenues designed a hundred and fifty years ago for a rising nation where "government by consent of the governed" could come into being. The streets and buildings were the same. The segregation laws hadn't changed. It was the people who were different. "Demopolis," she said, "a city of the people."

Though her position was purely advisory, without power and without pay, Mrs. Bethune had come prepared to work at it seriously. She took a small flat in a building that rented to Negroes and gathered about her the young men and women who had come from the colleges, from the cities, from the farms. They had come to work in the new Government agencies, on the staffs of organizations outside the Government, as taxi-drivers or waitresses, wherever work was to be had in this focal center of "a new world a-coming." The city was full of such young people—social workers, historians, teachers, for the first time in many generations called on to contribute their ideas and their skills. White and black, Southern and Northern, these were Mrs. Bethune's people.

They worked hard during the day. At night they sat at Mary Bethune's feet and planned for America's future. She called them her aides, but they called her Mother. To each of them, she gave the assurance, the security of being loved as an individual, so that under her influence they grew to be more themselves than they were before.

"I was more like a son to her," an important figure in the educational world of today recalls. "She loved me as if I were her own daughter," a prominent political figure explains. "Perhaps I oughtn't to say it, but I think I was Mother Bethune's favorite," says a third. Another of her "children,"—a teacher— writes: "She was nothing to look at, as I and others look at women. Her features were spread over her face as if in defiance of Western civilizations standards of beauty. One had to look within for the woman. Those who saw her with untainted vision shared, perhaps, her inward spirit. I think I was one of those who did."

They waited on her; they petted her; they learned from her. And they argued vigorously among themselves how best to use the new opportunities that were being opened. There was no difference in what they wanted. They wanted what the colored people in America have wanted through two hundred and fifty years of slavery and another ninety years of half-freedom: they wanted full exercise of citizenship, no more, no less. The arguments were about ways and means, about the special conditions of the North and the South. How far to bow to local prejudices? How fast to go in the fight for new patterns?

Each of the agencies had Negro advisers. Robert Weaver, William Trent Jr., Ira Reid, William Hastie, Jessie Fauset, Charles Johnson. No agency, at this period, had seen fit to give Negroes real power to act. Mrs. Bethune had come to Washington armed with her own program for using the National Youth Administration to carry on the "unfinished business" in the region she knew best. Now she saw that broader planning was needed, something that all the American people could build on. If there was a unified direction among the Negro people, more could be accomplished than even she had envisioned. She urged a conference of Negro leaders to talk out the problems.

"Racial cohesiveness," she said, "means making a rope of all the achievements of those who have had education until we reach the lowest person in the lowest stratum." It was in that spirit that the conference was held. It was a tremendous success and the forerunner of others.

Looking back on this opening period of the Roosevelt era, Charles Johnson, now President of Fisk University, estimated that greater advances were made in the march toward first-class citizenship for colored Americans than in any other single generation. Many factors entered into the change that took place. The times were propitious. Great impetus was given by a sympathetic and forceful President—and by his wife—in the White House. Nevertheless it remains true in our times as it was in the time of Frederick Douglass—liberty comes to the people who struggle for it. The greatest credit for the improvement of the condition of colored Americans must be given to the unity of direction Mary Bethune helped to forge at these conferences.

Recognition came from the Negroes themselves when, in 1935, Mrs. Bethune was awarded the Spingarn Medal. For twenty years this award had gone annually to the Negro "who had made the noblest achievement during the year."

The conference in Washington had been of great value. But she had a need to speak for great numbers. She missed the sense that she had as president of the National Association of Colored Women, of being a spokesman for Negro women everywhere.

"When I go before a committee of Congress and say that the poll tax has got to be repealed, they're not going to listen to plain Mary Bethune. But if I had the mandate to speak for the thousands North and South, perhaps they'd listen," she said to Mame Higgins. "*Individual* women banded together— hundreds of thousands of us—that is what's needed. Our voices could be like Joshua's trumpet. We'd blow down the walls that hem us in."

Wherever she went to consult about the slowly developing plans for the NYA, she talked with clubwomen, church leaders, lawyers, doctors, labor-organizers, teachers. She talked over her idea with Eleanor Roosevelt, with Mary Church Terrell, with the young Government workers who flocked to her shabby little apartment. She put her "aides" to writing letters—to gather a few representative women together in New York City to organize a National Council.

Mary Church Terrell nominated Mrs. Bethune for the presidency of the new organization. "We need a clubhouse where we can invite friends. We need rooms for interracial living."

Mary Bethune was dreaming big again. When she found a house on Vermont Avenue and proposed that the National Council of Negro Women buy it, everyone looked at her skeptically. A building in Washington costs money. Where would money like that come from?

"Never mind." Mrs. Bethune threw back her head and laughed. "I've got the 'somedays' That's what my sister used to call my impossible notions. If you agree that we need a clubhouse, God will help us get it."

Within a year the new organization had the building on Vermont Avenue. Among themselves, the small group of founders had raised $800 for a down payment. Mary Bethune had raised the rest of the money. The whole sum was the gift of Marshall Field. A total stranger, she had walked into his office in Chicago and come out triumphant, waving a check for $10,000.

The Council and its clubhouse did all its founder could have hoped for. The club became a meeting-place for the most forward-looking groups in American life. The National Council of Negro Women had thousands of members in its first year. Its membership now numbers almost a million.

Meanwhile the planning period for the National Youth Administration was coming to an end. Worthwhile projects had already been started. Over the country, thousands of young people between the ages of sixteen and twenty-four had been put to work at wages that at least paid for their food. They worked in libraries and public offices—cataloging, filing, checking records. They worked on the farms—plowing, harrowing, reaping. They graded, dumped, filled, drained to make roads in remote districts. They built dairy barns and country schools and playgrounds. The pattern of these projects followed closely the adult work plan of the WPA. In addition, girls' camps were set up in country places to restore their health and train them in cooking, sewing, and nursing. In all these projects Aubrey Williams and his colleague, Miss Roche, had insisted on allotment of funds to whites and Negroes alike without discrimination. In the North the young people worked side by side on NYA projects. In the South, where local laws required segregation the agency did its best to make the doctrine of "separate and equal" mean equal.

Still, Mrs. Bethune's plans for using the NYA for the special needs of the young people in the South were not yet fulfilled. Less than half of the young people who needed help were being used on the projects. The projects themselves, while useful enough, did not touch the matter of education.

She was only an advisor. She had no power to act; but she talked over her ideas with Aubrey Williams. There was a remarkable kinship and understanding between this rather solemn, thin-faced, gentle social worker and the dark-skinned, robust crusader. Both had known poverty and hard labor in their childhood; both carried memories of the same countryside—the soft, russet-colored winters, the smell of violets and wild honeysuckle in the swampy spring woods; the feel of hot dust on bare feet at berry-picking time; the sound of hickory nuts plopping to the earth and the noiseless drop of ripe persimmons after frost. When Mary Bethune talked about what she wanted to do for the country children of the South, Aubrey Williams understood.

The trouble was, he said, her plans would take money. Some Congressmen were already threatening to cut NYA appropriations. Some Southern newspapers were already bemoaning the favoritism toward the Negroes by the Roosevelt Administration—and by Mrs. Roosevelt.

"The fate of our people in America will be decided on the farms and crossroad towns in the Southern states," Mrs. Bethune answered. "Our mothers and fathers did not sacrifice and work and save for half-measures. They had to take crumbs. So did my generation. But crumbs are not good enough for our children and grandchildren."

"I know," Williams answered. "I think we'd better go see the President."

The Alabaman arranged for Mrs. Bethune to meet with President Roosevelt, to give a report on the first year's activities.

The conference was to take place in the evening, in Franklin Roosevelt's study. Mrs. Bethune prepared her report with a prayer in her heart, while her young friends with almost equal fervor pored over their wardrobes to see what they could lend her to wear. In borrowed finery, she set out with Aubrey Williams to meet the man who could open doors for millions of her people.

Mrs. Roosevelt was in the room and there were four or five others, but Mary Bethune kept her eyes fastened on the impressive figure of the President. She began with the formal report she had prepared, but soon the need, the great need of the children brushed away her awe. She forgot she was addressing the President of the United States. She talked about the boys and girls who had sacrificed so much to get an education and now couldn't use it. She talked about the children in the cabins who might never see the inside of a school. She talked about the hope the NYA could bring. "The $10 or $15 a month has saved lives," she said—and in her earnestness she shook her finger. "But you've got to do better than that for my people, Mr. President." Suddenly, she realized that she was lecturing the President of the United States as if he were one of her schoolboys. She apologized in embarrassment. Those who were present say that the President had tears in his eyes and Aubrey Williams whispered, as they left the White House:

"Thanks to you, Mrs. Bethune, a marvelous impression has been made for our cause."

Our cause . . . the cause of the Negro people and the cause of the South. They were one and inseparable. A few weeks after this meeting in Franklin Roosevelt's study, a new office was created in the NYA. Mary McLeod Bethune was made Director of Minority Affairs of the National Youth Administration.

Now all the experience Mrs. Bethune had gathered through the years, all her vision and genius for organization could be put to use. "Let those who can read teach those who cannot. Bring tents to set up in the field, even as the battles end," a freedman just a year out of slavery had begged Abraham Lincoln in 1864. "Let those who can read go out to teach the children who can't," Mary Bethune directed in 1936. At village crossroads, in the backwoods of the South, she set up schools without buildings, without formal curricula. The teachers were young men and women just out of school themselves. Under her inspiration, they gathered in the children of the sharecroppers who had no schools to go to, or the ones whose education had been cut short in the Depression. In the NYA schools, over the next few years, more than a million Negro children got the rudiments of an education. *Reading makes the difference!*

Mrs. Bethune's plans for education did not stop with reading and writing. She set up vocational training projects in agriculture, shop work, dressmaking. The young people were paid while they learned. The young teachers used the skills they had been in danger of forgetting. Girls with high-school or college training were put to organizing Mothers' clubs. Hundreds of the Bethune Mothers' clubs brought modern standards of health and child care to families living in back alleys in the cities or in unpainted shacks on the plantations. Nor was higher training forgotten. With the assistance of funds from the NYA, more than 40,000 young people were kept in the colleges and enabled to complete work for their degrees.

These years of Mary Bethune's life were among the happiest and most fruitful. Over sixty, troubled with a crippling asthma, which made sleeping and breathing difficult at times, she traveled over the country, looking for new situations where NYA projects could be helpful. She appointed and supervised the directors in the states and counties. She made hundreds of speeches. She somehow found time to give support and inspiration to every movement that gave promise of a better life for her people. She served as a vice-president of the NAACP; she helped Carter Woodson get funds to publish his *Journal of Negro History*. She met with people from all parts of the world—the colored of Asia and Africa. She was proudly an American and a Negro. But through all the activity, her major interest was the South.

In 1938, a small group of Southern educators and social workers called the first Conference for Human Welfare—an interracial meeting in the heart of Jim Crow country: Birmingham, Alabama. Many of the workers from Washington attended. Mrs. Roosevelt was one of the principal speakers. Mrs. Bethune went as a delegate from Florida. She, too, had a small place on the program.

The two friends happened to meet at the door of the hall where the conference was to be held. They had not seen each other for several weeks and had a dozen things to talk about. They came down the aisle, arm-in-arm, exchanging news of mutual interest.

Although the conference was an interracial affair, the laws of the city demanded segregation of the races. Policemen were on hand to see that Jim Crow got his due. Colored delegates were seated on one side of the aisle, white on the other. Mrs. Roosevelt and Mrs. Bethune walked the length of the hall. When they came to the front row facing the audience, without having to stop to think, Mrs. Bethune took her seat on the side of the room reserved for "colored." The wife of the President still had to be taught that lesson. She sat down next to Mary Bethune and continued talking.

A policeman stood at her shoulder. He coughed twice. Eleanor Roosevelt paid no attention. He tapped her on the shoulder. She might be the President's Lady, but here, Jim Crow was king.

It was a tense moment—for everyone except Eleanor Roosevelt. She calmly finished her anecdote, then moved her chair ever so little so that she was neither on the white side of the aisle nor on the black side. The policeman turned red in the face, but he made his way to the back of the hall. The somewhat flustered chairman rapped for order and the historic meeting was opened.

Mary Bethune looked around the room, recognizing many people she had worked with—teachers from Fisk and Atlanta University, women who had helped form the Southeastern Federation long years ago, young women who were members of the Council, a scattering of her own NYA supervisors.

There were a dozen other people in the hall whom she knew, but the thing that heartened her were the hundreds she did not know, men and women who had never before taken a prominent part in the struggle for equality. "The links are being forged," she thought. "Someday we will be one people—Americans."

Returning to Washington by train, Mrs. Bethune opened a magazine and saw a poem by young Langston Hughes. Idly she started to read:

O, let America be America again —
The land that never has been yet —
And yet must be — The land where every man is free.
The land that's mine —
The poor man's, Indians, Negro's, ME —
Who made America
Whose sweat and blood, whose faith and pain
Whose hand at the foundry, whose plow in the rain,
Must bring back our mighty dream again.

O, yes
I say it plain
America never was America to me
And yet I swear this oath —
America will be!
An ever-living seed
Its dream
Lies deep in the heart of me.

She let the slick pages slip out of her hands, her work-worn, gnarled, stubby hands. With a beautiful gesture left over from her childhood, her two hands met in prayer. "Dear Lord, let the time come quick. Don't you see, a boy like this young poet can't wait too long!   "

18. "Certain Unalienable Rights"

NIGHT AFTER NIGHT bombers and fighter planes headed east over the Potomac. At the clubhouse on Vermont Avenue, Mary Bethune, propped up in bed to make breathing easier, listened. It was the summer of 1943. America had been at war for more than a year.

Mrs. Bethune's work with the NYA was long finished. The agencies created to give work to the jobless of the Depression era had gone out of existence. Factories over the country were on twenty-four-hour shifts making materials for fighting. The cotton plantations, the farms were crying for "field hands." The young men and women who had gotten schooling and work experience in the National Youth Administration were in the factories, on the farms. And they were in the Army and Navy. Even before the United States entered the War with fighting forces, the industry and the allegiance of the country was deeply committed.

A year ago, Mrs. Bethune had seen that her work in Washington was coming to an end. She had prepared to return to Florida. She was tired and sick and she longed for her little cottage on the edge of Bethune-Cookman's magnificent campus. She had looked forward to becoming a teacher again. God meant her to teach. She wanted to make the day-to-day detailed decisions in the institution so uniquely her own.

There were seventeen buildings on the college campus now; thirty-one teachers (all of her own choosing), and almost seven hundred students. And Bethune-Cookman was in every sense a college, accredited with "A" rating by the Southern Association of Colleges and Secondary Schools, recognized as a center of education for *citizenship*.

It was no small job she had expected to go back to, as President of Bethune-Cookman. But the National Council of Negro Women had become of very real importance, too. The Council had about 800,000 members looking to her for leadership in the critical period after Pearl Harbor. She had stayed on in Washington for a few months, immersed in the affairs of the Council, in fund-raising for Carter Woodson's *Negro History Bulletin*, in the "March on Washington Movement," which (without a march) had won the Executive Order setting up a Fair Employment Practices Committee. (All of these things concerned her deeply and personally—she had belonged to the Association for the Study of Negro History since its beginning in 1916, and had been President since 1936. The March on Washington Movement was initiated by A. Philip Randolph—a former student at Cookman and one of her "boys." Aubrey Williams had helped formulate President Roosevelt's Executive Order 8802.)

Compelling as these interests were, Mary Bethune still had intended to go back to her college. Then the country, girding itself for a "war of survival," had called women into the Armed Forces. Enlistment in the Women's Army Corps—the WAC—was on a volunteer basis. Young Negro women by the thousands welcomed the opportunity to serve; but they wanted to serve to the *full* extent of their abilities. They did not want to be shunted off to menial jobs, discriminated against, belittled as their menfolk had been in the First World War. There was already tragic evidence that the same treatment might be repeated.

When a Texan, Mrs. Oveta Culp Hobby, was made head of the WAC, the Negro volunteers were worried. Could they expect fair treatment with a woman from the segregated South in charge? Committees, delegations, individuals besieged the War Department urging the appointment of someone to assist Mrs. Hobby to see that Americans of all races were accepted in the new corps as Americans. The National Council of Negro Women went farther. The members indicated the person they wanted— Mary McLeod Bethune. A few weeks later, Mrs. Bethune was offered the post of Special Civilian Assistant in the War Department.

Gone was the glimmering hope of quiet days in Florida. If there was an opportunity to see that young colored Americans had a chance to prove their worth, Mary Bethune was not one to hesitate. She resigned from the presidency of Bethune-Cookman and began the long, arduous struggle against Jim Crow in every branch of the Armed Forces. If the War Department expected the doughty old woman to be a safe figurehead they had a surprise in store. She let no opportunity pass to point out discrimination in any branch of the services. She was "Mother Bethune" to young men and women in the training camps, loving them, defending them with passionate energy, explaining their viewpoint to the President in the White House.

The response of the young people was touching. From Southern camps, from training bases in California, from ships in the Coral Sea, from Salvation Army huts in the African desert, from weather stations in Alaska, the letters came . . . hundreds of letters every month, and none went unanswered. The vibrating planes overhead that had wakened her were crossing to destinations unknown. But wherever airfields had been built to receive the planes, there were young Americans she knew and loved.

Some would not come home, but those who survived this war—what would they come back to? This was the question in the mind of every colored man and woman in America in 1943.

"We return. We return from fighting. We make way for democracy. We saved it in France and by the great Jehovah, we will save it in America or know the reason why." DuBois had said that in 1919. From 1919 to 1943 the zigzag battle to save democracy had gone on. And against indifference, against mobs, against all the odds, there had been progress.

"You can measure it," Mrs. Bethune said to herself, "by the present-day promises." The words spoken under stress of a second war were noble words: The Atlantic Charter, promising freedom and self-determination to nations, and the Four Freedoms of Franklin Roosevelt. The promises of a bright tomorrow were sweet to the ears of those who had waited so long for democracy to come their way. But already the promise of the Atlantic Charter was tarnished. When a West African leader—perhaps in very truth a kinsman of Mary Bethune—read about the pledge of national freedom, he wrote to the British Government, asking if this meant the freedom of Africa. A single sentence sufficed for Winston Churchill's answer: The Atlantic Charter applies only to the countries of Europe under the Nazi heel.

"Isn't Africa washed by the waters of the Atlantic?" Negroes asked, reading of the incident.

Colored men who had fought in the other war remembered how it was when they came home in 1919. Their women and children remembered how it was in the twenties—the decade of the Klan and the riots. Some of Mrs. Bethune's friends, when they heard the voice of the President promising *freedom from fear, freedom from want, freedom to speak, freedom to believe* turned their Bibles to the Book of James: "The tongue is a little member and boasts great things," they read. And farther on they read, "Faith without works is dead."

Two young stenographers in a War Labor Board office—one white, the other colored, were talking. "What do you think ought to be done with Hitler?" the white girl asked. "Paint him black and send him to Georgia," the other answered, and went on with her typing.

Rebellious youths in New York recited Richard Wright's verses:

I am black and I have seen black hands
Raised in fists of revolt, side by side with white fists of white workers—
And someday—and it is only this which sustains me—
Someday, there shall be millions and millions of them
On some red day in a burst of fists on a new horizon!

"The new horizons must come," the wakeful woman thought, in that summer night of 1943. "We who assume the responsibility of leadership must see that the raised fists are not needed. We don't work alone. We have allies at home—in the

White House itself. And by our side, the colored peoples of Africa and China and India."

She turned on the light, finding sleep impossible. On her night table was a pile of crisp typewritten sheets ready to go to the editor in the morning. Rayford Logan, Dean of the Graduate School of Howard University, was compiling a book: *What the Negro Wants*. He had asked her to contribute an essay.

When Dr. Logan came to talk over the volume with her, she had realized at once its importance. It could be a blueprint for the future. And it was to be published by the University of North Carolina Press at Chapel Hill. You had to be sixty-eight years old as she was— and born and educated and rooted in the South—to appreciate what it meant for them to bring out a book —not only by Negroes—but one in which the colored people stated their own needs and aspirations.

"The contributors are to have complete freedom of expression," Rayford Logan had said. "The publisher claims that he wants our honest opinions. He wants all shades represented."

Mrs. Bethune had glanced at her black face in a mirror and answered with a laugh. "What shade would you say I represent?"

She was always ready with a joke, but she had taken the writing of this essay very seriously, working it over and over again. She was once again a teacher, with an incoming class before her. The classroom was countrywide; the class, the whole of white America. A mixed group—some far advanced on the road of learning, needing only encouragement, ready to catch fire from a spark. There were some dullards, who had flunked the lessons of democracy over and over. There were some who needed to learn the ABC's of history.

This was a time and the opportunity, she felt, for plain speaking. Harmony between the races was needed against the challenge of fascism. But harmony was a white problem. They needed to realize that her people were only asking for the right to be Americans. The unalienable right. Unalienable, something so much a part of you that it could not be taken away—the unalienable American promise.

Unalienable—she remembered how both the sound and the sense of the word had opened vistas at Scotia. Fifty-four years ago, and she could still hear Miss Hattie Bowers saying it! Mrs. Bethune had called her essay "Certain Unalienable Rights." And she had begun it with the ABC's of American history as Miss Bowers had given it to her.

> Suddenly some rowboats move out from the shore. . . . The Boston Tea Party is in full swing. In this action a small and independent people struck out against restrictions and tyranny and oppression and gave initial expression to the ideal of a nation "that all men are created equal, that they are endowed by their Creator with certain unalienable rights."

It is a Sunday night in Harlem in the year of our Lord 1943. Along the quiet streets dimmed out against the possibility of Axis air attack, colored Americans move to and fro or sit and talk and laugh. Suddenly electric rumor travels from mouth to ear: "A black soldier has been shot by a white policeman and has died in the arms of his mother." No one stops to ask how or why or if it be true. Crowds begin to gather. There is a rumbling of anger and resentment impelled by all the anger and all the resentment of all colored Americans—the resentment against the mistreatment of Negroes in uniform, against restriction and oppression and discrimination— breaks loose. . . .

Some are saying that a band of hoodlums have challenged law and order to burn and pillage and rob. . . . [Others] will see depressed and repressed masses all over the world swelling to the breaking point against the walls of ghettos, against economic, social and political restrictions; they will find them breaking open the King's boxes and throwing tea into the ocean and storming Bastilles, stirred by the clarion call of the Four Freedoms.

They are rising to achieve the ideals "That all men are created equal, that they are endowed by their Creator with certain unalienable rights, that among these are Life, Liberty, and the pursuit of Happiness.". . . . They are part of a people's war. The little people want "out." Just as the Colonists at the Boston Tea Party wanted "out" under tyranny and oppression, the Chinese want "out," the Indians want "out," and colored Americans want "out."

They want release from so many different kinds of barriers. A barbed-wire enclosure came to Mary Bethune's mind and it wasn't in Nazi Germany. It was the barbed wire around the turpentine camp where she had founded the Bethune Mission. She thought of other barriers—the one she had met at Johns Hopkins a few years ago. She'd been ordered to the Baltimore hospital for an operation to help her breathing. The great medical institution had admitted her willingly—*but would not admit her doctor*. He was colored. God *had* let her do something about that! Negro doctors had been on the staff of Johns Hopkins from that time on. That was one wall she had helped to break down. But the barbed wire in Florida stood. Any complaints about it were called "agitation" and "stirring racial tension." Mrs. Bethune read farther down the page:

One who would really understand this racial tension which has broken out into actual conflict in riots as in Harlem, Detroit, and Los Angeles, must look to the roots and not be confused by the branches and the leaves. The tension rises out of the growing internal pressure of Negro masses to break through the wall of restriction which restrains them from full American citizenship. This mounting power is met by the unwillingness of white America to allow any appreciable breach in this wall. . . . They need no agitation by newspaper accounts or the stimulation of so-called leaders. These things are the intimate experiences of the masses themselves. They know them and feel them intensely and resent them bitterly.

A book snatched from the hand of a child. "You can't read, you're black!" Mary Bethune could see that cruel, childish gesture, now, as a historical hangover of slavery. To maintain slavery the master race had to teach that Negroes were inferior beings. She could understand and write about the situation with a degree of objectivity. But the scars inflicted by the whites had gone deep.

They met every effort on [the Negroes'] part to break through these barriers with stern resistance that would brook no challenge to our concept of white supremacy. Although they guaranteed him full citizenship under the Constitution and its Amendments, they saw to it that he was largely disfranchised and had little part in our hard-won ideal of "the consent of the governed."

In the midst of this anachronism, they increasingly educated his children in the American way of life—in its ideals of equality of all men before the law, and opportunities for the fullest possible development of the individual.

As this concept took hold among the Negro masses, it has evidenced itself through the years in a slow, growing, relentless pressure against every restriction which denied them their full citizenship. This pressure, intensified by those of other races who really believed in democracy, began to make a break through the walls here and there. It was given wide-spread impetus by the objectives of the New Deal with its emphasis on the rise of the forgotten man.

The people of good will had made an enormous difference—the Roosevelts, Aubrey Williams, Pearl Buck, Oscar Chapman, Lillian Smith, and the hundreds of others. Mary Bethune thought of her friends with gratitude. But she was aware that definite steps had to be taken. Her eyes ran down the typewritten pages. Had she made all the points and made them clearly?

Government leadership in building favorable public opinion. The President himself had done much. Mary Bethune constantly saw his influence as she and Eleanor Roosevelt traveled over the country, often together, speaking to huge audiences to help win the War. The man in the White House should lead, but a special federal agency was needed. The cost of segregation and discrimination came too high to a nation at war. And victory of democracy over dictatorship was vital. Experience taught only too well the implications for the Negro of a Nazi victory. To win that victory, there must be *democracy in the Armed Forces*. Mrs. Bethune read on.

> *The protection of [the Negro's] civil rights and an end to lynching.* He wants full protection of the rights guaranteed all Americans by the Constitution; equality before the law, the right to jury trial and service, the eradication of lynching. Demanding these rights for himself, he will not be misled into any anti-foreign, red-baiting, or anti-Semitic crusade to deny these rights to others. Appalled by the conditions prevailing in Washington, he joins in demanding the ballot for the District of Columbia and the protection of his rights now denied him within the shadow of the Capitol.

The Free ballot and Extension of federal programs in public housing, health social security, education and relief under federal control.

Mary Bethune saw in her mind's eye the pleasant, low-cost homes that had replaced some of the shacks at Daytona Beach. She could not help but feel proud to have helped get that project started. But without the Federal Government the shacks and the outhouses would not have been torn down. She read carefully her statement of the reasons for the nation as a whole to take the responsibility for human welfare.

> Low income and local prejudice often deprive [the Negro] of these basic social services. Private enterprise or local government units cannot or will not provide them. For efficiency and equity in administration of these programs, the Negro looks to the federal government until such time as he has gained the full and free use of the ballot in all states.

Equal access to employment opportunities. Elimination of racial barriers in labor unions. The one must go hand-in-hand with the other. Negro youth must have an equal chance to be trained. Her people must have a fair share of public jobs. Job control on public works must be denied to any union practicing discrimination.

Realistic interracial cooperation. [The Negro] realizes the complete interdependence of underprivileged white people and Negroes, North and South—laborers and sharecroppers alike. He knows that they stay in the gutter together or rise to security together; that the hope of democracy lies in their cooperative effort to make their government responsive to their needs; that national unity demands their sharing together more fully in the benefits of freedom—not "one as the hand and separate as the fingers," but one as the clasped hands of friendly cooperation.

Here then was a program—not just for the Negro himself but for national unity. Mary Bethune was satisfied, reading it over, that it added up to the sum of things needed. There had remained to show her people themselves how they could help get what they wanted.

In the first place, we must see to it the "white and Negroes alike understand the current intensity of the Negro's fight for status as part of a world people's movement."

SECONDLY: We must challenge, skillfully but resolutely, every sign of restriction or limitation on our full American citizenship. When I say challenge, I mean we must seek every opportunity to place the burden of responsibility upon him who denies it. If we simply accept and acquiesce in the face of discrimination, we accept the responsibility ourselves and allow those responsible to salve their conscience by believing that they have our acceptance and concurrence. We should, therefore, protest openly everything in the newspapers, on the radio, in the movies that smacks of discrimination or slander. We must take the seat that our ticket calls for and place upon the proprietor the responsibility of denying it to us.

We must challenge everywhere the principle and practice of enforced racial segregation. . . .

Our appeal must be made to the attributes of which the Anglo-Saxon is so proud—his respect for law and justice, his love of fair-play and true sportsmanship.

THIRD: We must understand that the great masses of our people are farmers and workers, and that their hopes for improvement in a large measure lie in association with organizations whose purpose is to improve their condition. This means membership in and support of labor and farmer unions. . . . The voice of organized labor has become one of the most powerful in the land and unless we have a part in that voice our people will not be heard.

FOURTH: We must take a full part in the political life of our community, state and nation. . . . This is a representative government and the only way that our representatives can reflect our desires is for us to register and vote.

Register and vote. Mary Bethune thought of Frank Wilson on the night the Klan marched. Frank Wilson and all the men and women who had marched with her to drop their votes in the ballot box. That was a long time ago. Her stride had been as long as a man's then. Now she walked with a cane and was glad of an arm to lean on; but if God was willing she would continue to lead men and women to the polls as long as she lived.

Especially the women. Hers would be the only woman's voice represented in Rayford Logan's book. She had protested. There were plenty of women as capable of speaking as the men.

"There's a limit to the length of a book," he had answered. And he depended on her to give the woman's viewpoint.

Negro women and their organization have a tremendous responsibility and opportunity to offer leadership and support to this struggle of the racial group to attain improved cultural status in America. We have always done a full part of this job. . . . We feel behind us the surge of all women of China and India and of Africa who see the same light and look to us to march with them. We will reach out our hands to all women who struggle forward—white, black, brown, yellow—all. If we have the courage and tenacity of our forebears, who stood firmly like a rock against the lashings of slavery and the disruption of Reconstruction, we shall find a way to do for our day what they did for theirs. Above all we Negro women of all levels and classes must realize that this forward movement is a march of the masses and that all of us must go forward with it or be pushed aside by it. We will do our part. In order for us to have peace and justice and democracy for all, may I urge that we follow the example of the great humanitarian—Jesus Christ—in exemplifying in our lives both by work and action the fatherhood of God and the brotherhood of man?

Mary Bethune laid the manuscript down. She was afraid the editor of the University of North Carolina Press wasn't going to like what she had written. But he was going to print it, nevertheless. That was the great thing.

"Twenty years ago," she said to herself, "that couldn't have happened. A Southern editor wouldn't have cared to know what we wanted."

19. "We, the People of the United Nations"

"We have learned to be citizens of the world," President Roosevelt said in his Fourth Inaugural Address on January 20, 1945. The ceremony took place out of doors on the steps of the South Portico of the White House. It was a cold, blustery day, but Mrs. Bethune had insisted on coming to see the man she revered take the oath of office for a fourth term. She knew that the votes of the Negro people (where they were permitted to vote) had helped to keep Roosevelt in the White House and she was proud.

She walked slowly across the crowded White House grounds, breathing with difficulty and leaning on her cane. She had to admit to herself these days that her enormous fund of energy and strength was waning. But she forgot her own illness at the sight of the President, standing without hat or overcoat, his pitiful, useless legs supported by heavy steel braces and two canes. He looked so tired and worn and thin that Mrs. Bethune was shocked. During her years in Washington she had come to feel deep personal affection for the President and she had the conviction that he liked her in return. He seemed to enjoy her frankness and matched her zest and supreme self-confidence with his own. The bond between them was based on a common practicality and common sense but it was also a bond of deep spiritual belief in the duty of man to fulfill God's purposes.

The inaugural ceremony was very short. An occasion which might have been used to celebrate the tremendous military triumphs of the past year was used instead to dedicate the minds of the people to the future.

France was wholly liberated. The "Red Ball Express" was rolling ever closer to the meeting place with the Russian armies in the heart of Germany. This transport division—the truckers who kept the life-line of supplies open in the forward sweep across Europe—was composed largely of Negro troops. Their letters to Mary Bethune were no longer filled with anxiety and frustration. The "Red Ball Express" was exultant. To be useful and used! From the highest to the lowest, this was the thing that counted. It would please the President to know about these letters. It would hearten him to know that these young men, too, had found themselves as citizens of the world.

The inaugural ceremony was very short. Roosevelt's speech had lasted no more than five minutes. Mrs. Bethune walked away from the crowd unaccountably depressed. The President needed rest, but how would he get it with the fears and hopes of hundreds of millions of people bearing down on him? She knew that he was preparing to go across the ocean for one of the fateful conferences with Prime Minister Churchill and Marshal Stalin. Always before, the conferences had concerned themselves with waging war—this one was for ending the fighting and "waging" peace.

Early in 1942, with his creative instinct for phrase-making, Franklin Roosevelt had given the name "United Nations" to the countries engaged in battle against Hitler and his allies. In the last year, the name had become a symbol of the unity that was being built for a world at peace. The plans for a permanent organization were far advanced. For months, Government representatives worked at Dumbarton Oaks on the outlines. Problems which only the top leadership could solve would be ironed out in the coming conference at Yalta. The place and time would be set for the meeting of all the nations to formulate a charter.

Mrs. Bethune, like every Negro leader in the country, was afire with the idea. The colored peoples of the world, the people of China and India, the colonial peoples of the rest of Asia and of Africa were drawing together. Colored Americans saw their needs as part of the world problem. The treatment of fourteen million Americans would no longer be a private affair. It was equally true that American Negroes could make a great contribution toward cementing the kinship of nations. The creation of a United Nations organization even before the war ended would mark the dawning of a new day.

Mrs. Bethune was devoting her whole attention to putting the idea of the United Nations before the people with whom she had contact. She wrote letters and articles, she prepared speeches. But she could not get her concern for the President out of her mind. She had a great desire to see him before he left for his long journey. When she phoned for an appointment, his secretary made room at once on the crowded White House calendar. "The President always likes to see you, Mrs. Bethune," she said. "You never ask for anything for yourself."

Mary Bethune got through with what she wanted to say very quickly. She had no serious problems, she just wanted to assure him that the hearts of her people went with him on his journey. Then she came around to his chair and took his hands in her own. No word was spoken between them. But her eyes were filled with tears as she hurried from the room. Mary Bethune never saw the President again.

He returned from the Yalta Conference with the plans for the meeting of nations completed. San Francisco was to be the place, the time April 25, 1945 just a little over two months away.

The official United States delegates were chosen. But there were also to be unofficial "observers," representing all the important groups and organizations in the country. The observers were expected to play a part in interpreting the new world organization to the American people. The President, Mrs.

Roosevelt said, was depending on people like Mrs. Bethune, as head of the National Council of Negro Women, to make an important contribution to the success of the conference.

Once before, when the League of Nations was formed, America had had a chance to take its place of world leadership for peace. The Congress had voted to stay out of the League of Nations. Great care was being taken that this should not happen again.

Franklin Roosevelt made another speech before going to his cottage at Warm Springs, Georgia, to rest until the opening of the San Francisco Conference. Mrs. Bethune was in the South on a speaking tour. She read the Jefferson Day speech of the President over and over. As usual he had said the right words at the right time: "Today we are faced with the preeminent fact that if civilization is to survive, we must cultivate the science of human relationships—the ability of all peoples, of all kinds, to live together and work together in the same world, at peace."

Mrs. Bethune was in Dallas, Texas, at the home of friends, when the news came over the radio that the President was dead.

Two days later she was in the East Room of the White House with the hundred or more of the President's personal friends who had come to attend the simple funeral service. The President was dead. There was nothing to do, nothing to say. The roomful of people sat dumb.

Mrs. Roosevelt came in, quiet, composed, full of dignity. The time of their first meeting came to Mary Bethune's mind. I pray to God to give me the courage to change what can be changed, the serenity to accept what cannot he changed. . . . She wept unashamedly. She wept for her friend's loss and her own and for all those gathered in that room. She wept for the millions in the land, her own people on the farms, in the factories and mines, on the battlefields. The President was dead. They would all have to learn to accept that. But the dignity, the self-respect they had won with the help of Franklin Roosevelt could never be taken away.

Two weeks after Roosevelt was buried, the conference to bring into being his plan for a United Nations organization was scheduled to open. Last-minute arrangements were undertaken with frenzied haste. The list of selected organizations invited to send representatives to San Francisco had been published. The National Council of Negro Women was not on the list.

"An oversight," someone in the State Department said, when Mrs. Roosevelt called to find out what had happened. A regrettable oversight, but to add even one more organization would be to reopen the whole list. Dozens of other groups were also disappointed. It seemed the whole population of the United States wanted to attend the conference.

"Mrs. Bethune must go to San Francisco," Eleanor Roosevelt replied. "She is needed."

The National Association for the Advancement of Colored People had been invited to send three observers. Two representatives had been named: Walter White, the executive secretary of the organization, and Dr. W. E. B. DuBois. Mary McLeod Bethune was a vice-president of the NAACP. She was invited to go as the third representative. She accepted with grace but with some hesitancy, aware that her appointment by the NAACP deprived some more active leader of participation. If the National Council of Negro Women had been included, her people would have had additional representation.

Once arrived at San Francisco, Mrs. Bethune put aside her disappointment and looked for opportunities for usefulness. The interest in the conference was intense. The beautiful city was crowded, the conference hall besieged at every session by hundreds more spectators than could be admitted. Special meetings were arranged, after each session, where the observers could give their detailed impressions to the public. Mrs. Bethune's charm, her keen insight and eloquence made her a favorite speaker at these meetings.

As she had expected, the Negro people showed an extraordinary interest in the proceedings. They looked to the international organization as a weapon against discrimination in their own country. Every Negro newspaper in America had sent a correspondent. Each clause in the charter was eagerly studied as it was adopted—not only for its bearing on the problems of the colored people in America but of oppressed minorities over the world.

Mrs. Bethune did not bring to the analysis of the charter the profound knowledge of Dr. DuBois. She could not speak with the authority of Dr. Ralph Bunche in his capacity of the State Department's acting chief of the Division of Dependent Territories. But she could inspire people with her abiding faith, she could give them warmth and wisdom.

Mary Bethune was eternally a teacher. In San Francisco, during the conference, her classroom was the whole world, her pupils, mankind. Words like human dignity and equal rights were not to her mere phrases. The clauses agreed on in the conference-room came to life when she reported them.

"We, the peoples of the United Nations, determined . . . to reaffirm faith in fundamental human rights, in the dignity and worth of the human person, in the equal rights of men and women and of nations large and small."

Human dignity as she explained it was small courtesies such as giving each person the title that belonged to him by right and custom. It was jobs under decent working conditions and the right to be served in a restaurant, to buy a house where you wanted to live. It was respect for language and beliefs and traditions unlike your own. It was the right to be different.

"I don't mind being different," she said. "I don't want to be Jim-Crowed to a back seat because I'm black and I don't want to be ushered to a front seat because I'm not white so they can 'palaver' over me."

The conference lasted two months. There were deep-seated political differences and tense moments when it seemed that the dream of an organization for peace in the midst of war would fail. Roosevelt's exceptional qualities of leadership were almost fatally missed. However, the cause of peace and the advancement of democracy does not depend on one man. The peoples of the world needed the United Nations too urgently to allow it to fail.

On the 26th of June the final clauses of the charter were agreed upon. The impressive ceremony of the signing of the charter by the representatives of the nations took place. The conference came to an end.

On one of the last days, Mrs. Bethune and Eleanor Roosevelt had a quiet moment together. Mary Bethune spoke of the President, of the admiration she had for him. She wanted, she said, something of his that she could keep close to her always.

"He said I never asked for anything for myself. But now I ask it. Give me one of his canes."

It was a strange request, but the gift of the cane clearly meant a great deal to Mrs. Bethune. She was never without it, to the end of her life. Perhaps it was a symbol to her of Franklin Roosevelt's courage under great difficulties, for she knew that out of suffering had come understanding and sympathy for all the oppressed people of the world.

20. A Year and a Day

Insofar as a person with Mary Bethune's zest for living could be said to retire, her seventy-fifth birthday, on July 19, 1950, marked her retirement. She had resigned from the presidency of the National Council of Negro Women and from the presidency of the Association for the Study of Negro Life and History. The cottage on the Bethune-Cookman campus had once more become home to her. As President-Emeritus of the college, Dr. Bethune added prestige and, it must be confessed, a bit of spice to the campus life. She no longer strode across the campus in a white dress like an avenging angel to pick up a fallen leaf or a scrap of paper. She no longer tacked handwritten mottoes on the academic walls. She walked very slowly now, leaning on the gold-headed cane that had belonged to Franklin Roosevelt; or she sat quietly in her study surrounded by mementos of the amazing number of careers she had managed to crowd into a lifetime. The college felt her presence, nevertheless. There was not one of the fifty faculty members, scarcely one of the eight hundred students but felt the inspiration of "Mother Bethune."

To be invited to her study to examine the inscribed photographs of the world's great men and women was a coveted privilege. A whole period of history was in those photographs and in the medals, the citations of honorary degrees, the mementos of her journeys to Haiti, to Europe, and, miraculously, to Africa, as America's representative at the inauguration of the President of Liberia.

A faded portrait of Lucy Laney hung on the wall; another of Mary Crissman; snapshots of Mrs. Bethune's grandchildren and of her great-grandchildren. President Roosevelt's portrait was there, and a favorite one of Eleanor Roosevelt, Mary Bethune, and Mme. Pandit of India, taken at the magnificent birthday dinner in New York in July of 1950. There was a portrait of the President of Haiti and one of Aubrey Williams. Marian Anderson's picture was there, taken soon after the Lincoln Memorial Concert back in 1939. And Roland Hayes, who had come down to Bethune-Cookman to sing at the Thirty-fifth Anniversary celebration that same year. There was a photograph of Mary Church Terrell, and of one of the tribal kings of Nigeria, whose son was one of the African students at the college.

There was the Spingarn Medal from the NAACP and the Frances A. Drexel Award given in 1936 "for distinguished service to her race"; the medal from the National Association of Negro Musicians, and the Thomas Jefferson Medal from the Southern Conference for Human Welfare, bestowed in 1942.

There were the citations of Dr. Bethune's honorary degrees— the first from the State College of her own South Carolina, then from Tuskegee and Wilberforce, from the State College of Arkansas, from Xavier, Bennett, Morris Brown and Wiley; degrees from Lincoln and Howard and Atlanta Universities; and the last, from Rollins College in Florida.

To Mary Bethune, this degree of Doctor of Humanities conferred in 1949 was a source of special pride, not because she was the first colored woman to be recognized in this way by a Southern institution for whites but because the honor signified the relationship she had been able to establish between Florida colleges, Negro and white. For the last five years the Florida Intercollegiate Interracial Conferences had met at Bethune-Cookman for discussion and study of their mutual problems. Every year, for a few days at least, a few young Southerners disregarded the color line. They sat down together, seeking to cultivate the science of human relationships, without which, as President Roosevelt had once said, civilization could not survive.

Mary Bethune liked to look up from her desk and see all these mementos. She liked to show them to visitors. They were symbols of the march of democracy—the black faces and the white faces and the brown faces together. We are on the right path. We have set our direction. We will reach our goal.

On a night in January 1952, however, Dr. Bethune was not looking at the photographs of world-famous artists and statesmen. She held in her hand a photograph of a fellow Floridian, Harry T. Moore. A newspaper was spread out before her and she scanned the pages anxiously, looking for some small paragraph, somewhere, that would give encouragement that something was being done about the murder of Harry Moore and his wife, Harriet. Three weeks had passed since the ancient shadow of an ancient wrong had fallen once more on her people—this time in Florida. On Christmas night, the Moores' house had been bombed. Harry Moore had died instantly; Harriet Moore had lived, mortally wounded, for a few days longer—long enough to attend her husband's funeral on a stretcher, long enough to whisper to officials the names of the suspected murderers. Both the Moores had been teachers. And Mrs. Bethune had sat with them often in NAACP meetings, working out means and methods for the advancement of democracy, for breaking down discrimination and segregation, for helping the people of Florida to learn to live together.

That was their crime, that they believed in democracy. Harry Moore had been state head of the NAACP. He had passed out leaflets in favor of the Fair Employment Practices Committee. He had sent questionnaires to political candidates regarding their views on segregation. Such little things, but enough ....

No arrests had been made. Mary Bethune pushed the newspaper aside. No arrests would be made. The telegrams and protests pouring in from the rest of the country were not going to move the Florida authorities to act. What was all the fuss about? Just a couple of "uppity niggers" who were getting along all right before they started stirring up trouble?

The people who killed Harry Moore hadn't hated him as a person. They hadn't even known him or Mrs. Moore. How could they, with the force of law raised as a wall between them?

Here in the South, the homeland of her people, one more man and woman, two fine people, had been killed. But the battle would have to go on here and everywhere. *If civilization is to survive we have to learn to live together and work together — all kinds of people, all over the world.*

At the dinner arranged in honor of her seventy-fifth birthday, back in 1950, Mrs. Bethune had said. "Peace and understanding can only be realized by creating the conditions under which democracy can thrive." Now peace had become a word that was put in quotation marks in the newspapers. People like Dr. DuBois who dared to speak their opinions—right or wrong— were charged with being foreign agents. Dr. DuBois, that grand old scholar of eighty-four years, was arrested and brought into court in handcuffs. The voices of Paul Robeson, Canada Lee, and dozens of other Negro artists were silenced in the theater and on the radio for being dissenters. Mrs. Bethune herself had been denied the platform in a public school in Englewood, New Jersey. This was an infinitesimal thing compared to what was happening to others, but it had been a sign—a bad sign.

The attack on Mary Bethune, the humiliation of Dr. DuBois had roused public opinion, Negro and white. Dr. DuBois had been released and was later acquitted. Dr. Bethune had spoken in Englewood. Democracy in America was not dead. Struggle only made it grow stronger.

Ralph Bunche had put his finger on the reason democracy was worth fighting for: "The practical essence of a democratic society is in the mechanisms it affords for the solutions of its problems."

One of these mechanisms was the United States Supreme Court, through which the laws of the land could be made to, conform to the Constitution and the Amendments. Since its founding, the NAACP had turned to the courts for remedy against injustice to the Negro people. It is a great thing to have the law of the land on the side of justice and liberty. Slowly, over the years, decisions of the Supreme Court had broken down the wall of segregation behind which the rights of citizenship could be denied.

Now a campaign was on to break down the wall at its very base: segregation of children in the public schools. The battle was long. It was fought on many fronts. There were five cases brought up from courts in many parts of the country—the most crucial, the case from Clarendon County, South Carolina, where

Negro parents risked their jobs and their safety to sign petitions requesting admission of their children to schools reserved for whites. A Southern judge, Justice Waties Waring, had supported the petition—for which action rocks had been thrown through the windows of his Charleston home.

Now, Thurgood Marshall and his colleagues of the NAACP had presented the five cases to the United States Supreme Court. In 1952 the Court deferred decision. Nineteen hundred and fifty-three came and went. The time was not spent in passive waiting. There was a whole country to be taught the significance of the cases to America and to the world.

Mary Bethune worked and watched. She spoke; she wrote. She used every technique of her long experience to get her people ready to implement the decision if it should prove favorable. She saw that the South would be the battleground. She was no longer physically strong enough to bear the brunt of leadership, but she had raised up legions.

"I'll never rest," she said, "never as long as there is a single Negro boy or girl without the chance that every human being deserves—the chance to prove his worth."

Walter White consulted her; Mrs. Roosevelt kept her informed. Members of the National Council of Negro Women stood ready.

It was on May 17, 1954 that the unanimous decision of the Supreme Court was published to a waiting world: Segregation according to color was inconsistent with the provisions of the

Constitution. The states of the United States were directed to proceed to desegregate the public schools "with all reasonable speed."

Chief Justice Warren, who wrote the decision, had been appointed to the Court by President Eisenhower. Two other judges had been appointed by Truman. Five were Roosevelt appointees. Three of the judges were from Southern states where segregation was in force.

Mary McLeod Bethune was almost seventy-nine years old, and weak from long illness; but on that day in the spring of 1954 she strode across the campus swinging her cane. She moved with the strength that victory brings to an old warrior.

"Sing" she commanded the group of young students who surrounded her. And she led them in a voice whose tone still held something of its beauty:

Rise and shine and give God the glory . . .

Glory for the Year of Jubilee!

None of the Negro leaders, least of all Dr. Bethune, thought the battle for full citizenship was over. But the courts had spoken, the decision of May 17 had established a principle that segregation is of itself the form and essence of discrimination. Jim Crow had been struck a mortal blow.

There were all sorts of matters to be considered, arguments to be met. There was the admitted ill-preparedness of colored children who had been given schooling unequal in equipment, in buildings, in pay for teachers. Children in some places would for a time suffer genuine hardship. "But," said Mary Bethune, "it is a tortuous logic that would use the tragic result of inequality to establish the need for continuing it."

There was the problem of the teachers. Sixty-five per cent of the students at Bethune-Cookman were preparing to teach. Rumors were rampant in colleges like Bethune-Cookman that thousands of colored teachers in the South would lose their jobs. Mrs. Bethune marshalled facts and figures to show that the need for teachers was such that this was not likely to happen.

There was the further question of continuing support for the Negro colleges. While she was living in Washington, Mrs. Bethune had been active in launching the United Negro College Fund. This foundation, proposed by Dr. F. D. Patterson, of Tuskegee Institute, had undertaken successfully to raise funds for the running expenses of the group of major colleges for Negroes. William Trent Jr., one of her "boys," was director of the Fund. He was not worried about the fate of these needed centers of education.

Lastly, there was the question of acceptance of the decision by the white Southerners, imprisoned as they were in the walls of their own taboos. Mrs. Bethune quoted an old African proverb: *If you know well the beginning, the end will not trouble you much.* She had confidence in the future but she wished the future would hurry up!

On the 24th of July, 1954, the news came of Mary Church Terrell's death.

"She lived to hear the decision," Dr. Bethune said thankfully. She had lived, too, to see Washington theaters and restaurants opened up by President Eisenhower's desegregation order.

A few months later, Mary Mason died. She had been ill a long time, and Mame Mason Higgins had gone home to live with her. Mame came down that winter to spend a few weeks at Bethune-Cookman.

"Thank God Mama lived to hear the decision!" she said, as they talked lovingly of Mary Mason.

Mrs. Bethune was aware, without her doctor's telling her, that the future would be in the hands of others. On the last day of Mame's visit, they were sitting in the study. Mrs. Bethune spread her hands in a large, generous gesture that was so characteristic.

"I'd like you to have some of my things," she said, in an offhand, matter-of-fact way. "Pictures, statues, jewels, that fur coat you like, anything—except my cane."

Mame shook her head, her eyes bright with tears. Mother Bethune had given her the precious thing, the proud knowledge of what it is to be a Negro, the inheritance of a great history, the understanding that comes from suffering, the growth of the human soul through struggle.

This was Mame's last glimpse of Dr. Bethune. The long span of her life came quietly to an end on May 18, 1955—ninety-two years after the Emancipation Proclamation, a year and a day after the historic Supreme Court decision.

This then is the story of Mary McLeod Bethune. Her birth was recorded nowhere; the notices of her death appeared on the front pages of newspapers over the country. Many people in America and in Africa and in Asia wrote eulogies praising her. The *Journal of Negro History* said:

> Mary McLeod Bethune was a leader who rose from the strength of her great ability and was the unquestioned choice of those whom she inspired and led. . . . She was statesmanlike, long before she laid down her sword and shield, to pass her torch to others. . . . She lived devoutly before her God and in rare consecration to all mankind. Her crown reserved for the righteous and valiant is won.

But perhaps the place held in our country's history by Mary McLeod Bethune, an American and a Negro, is best set forth in the words of a young girl in a Louisville, Kentucky, high school a few years ago. She was asked what Negro leader, man or woman, she would most like to be. She answered:

"I would prefer to be Mrs. Bethune, because she is the most outstanding, and has worked harder than any of them to get what she wanted.   "

Index

Augusta, Georgia

Fair Employment Practices Committee

Faith Hall (Daytona)

Faith Hall (Scotia)

Fauset, Jessie

Field, Marshall

Fisk Jubilee Singers

Fisk University

Flagler, Henry

Florida Intercollegiate InterracialConferences

Four Freedoms

Franklin, Benjamin

Freedmen's Bureau

freedom, petitions for

Gabriel

Gamble, James N.

Garrison, William Lloyd

Godey's Lady's Book

Greeley, Abby

Guinea Africa

Haines Normal and Industrial Institute

Haiti

Hamburg, S.C. massacre

Hampton Choir

Hampton Industrial Institute

Harlem riots

Hastie, William

Hayes, Roland

Higgins, Mame Mason

Hitler, Adolf

History of the Negro

Hobby, Oveta Culp

Hopkins, Harry

Howard University

Hughes Langston, quoted Hunter College hymns

    "My Soul Is Anchored in the Lord"

    significance of in Negro history

    sung at Bethune Missions

    "Year of Jubilee"

illiteracy (see also literacy)

    among Negroes

    among Southern whites

interracial cooperation

    conferences concerning

    in fight against lynching

    in fight for women's suffrage

    influence of white teachers in South

    during Reconstruction

    support of schools by white people

    in Urban League

London, England

L'Ouverture, Toussaint

Loving, Bertha

lynching

Macon, Ga.

Madison, James

March on Washington Movement

Marshall, Thurgood

Mason, Madison C. B.

Mason, Mame, *see Higgins, Mame*

Mason Mason, Mary (Mrs. Madison)

Mayesville Mission School

Mayesville, S.C.

McClellan, Rose

McDowell, Mary

McLeod Castle

McLeod, Hattie

National Urban League

National Youth Administration (NYA)

Negro history; Association for Study of; at Daytona School; distortion of; role of spirituals in

Negro History Bulletin

Negro people

in American Revolution

in Civil War

suffering of during Depression

in World War I

in World War II

Negro people's organizations *see* Equal Suffrage League;

National Association for Advancement of Colored People

National Association of Negro Musicians

National Association of Negro Women

United Negro College Fund

United States Supreme Court *see* Supreme Court

Vermont first state to emancipate slaves

Vesey, Denmark

vocational training

Volusia County

voter's club

voting *see* suffrage

Walker, Carrie

Waring, Waties

War Department

War Labor Board

Warm Springs, Ga.

Warren, Earl

Washington, Booker T. quoted

Washington, D.C.

A NOTE ON THE AUTHOR

Emma Gelders Sterne was born in Birmingham, Alabama. When told to write about the place she knew best she was confronted with a problem. In her own words: "A white Southerner grew up knowing only half of the South. Knowledge of conditions under which the other half lived was denied her."

While Mrs. Sterne lived in the South, she never heard the name of Mary McLeod Bethune. Not until years later did she hear the eloquent voice, read the words filled with tolerance and compassion, sit in the same room and concern herself with the same problems. Like thousands of other Americans, Mrs. Sterne quickly came under the spell of this dynamic woman.

Mrs. Sterne, author of numerous successful junior historical novels, also wrote adult books. She was a teacher, a freelance writer, and an editor of children's books. She made her home in San Jose, California, and spent much of her time writing and enjoying her two children and nine grandchildren.

Made in the USA
Columbia, SC
24 March 2020